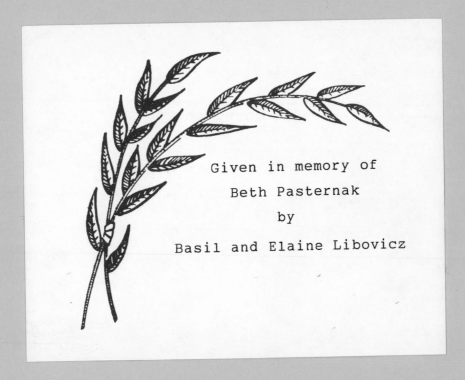

Given in memory of
Beth Pasternak
by
Basil and Elaine Libovicz

Cakes by Design

"EVERLASTING"

Cakes by Design

THE MAGICAL WORLD OF SUGAR ART

Scott Clark Woolley

and

Michael G. Farace

THE OVERLOOK PRESS
WOODSTOCK • NEW YORK

To Ralph and Louise Woolley,
whose generous support helped us
turn this dream into a reality

First published in the United States in 1997 by
The Overlook Press
Lewis Hollow Road
Woodstock, New York 12498

Library of Congress Cataloging-in-Publications Data

Woolley, Scott Clark.
Cakes by design: the magical world of sugar art / Scott Clark Woolley,
Michael G. Farace.
Includes index.
1. Sugar art. 2. Cake decorating. I. Farace, Michael. G.
II. Title
TX799.W67   1996   641.8'653—dc20   96-89

Photographs and Illustrations by Scott Clark Woolley and Michael G. Farace

BOOK DESIGN AND FORMATTING BY BERNARD SCHLEIFER

Printed in the United States of America

First Edition

ISBN 0-87951-674-7

10 9 8 7 6 5 4 3 2 1

SPECIAL NOTE

All the cakes included in this book were genuine cakes, not dummies, with the
exception of "A Dream Come True," "Showers of Happiness," and "Still Life," which
were constructed for permanent display.

Contents

*"Just living is not enough," said the butterfly.
"One must have sunshine, freedom,
  and a little flower."*

HANS CHRISTIAN ANDERSEN

Acknowledgments

Many kind souls have helped and guided us along the way toward the publication of this book. From our hearts, we express our deepest appreciation to:

Joan Raines, our literary agent, for her tireless commitment, enthusiasm, and loving care;

Larry Ritter, author and friend, who graciously opened the door to Raines & Raines;

Tracy Carns, our astute editor, whose vision so easily melded with our own, and the entire team at The Overlook Press, particularly Bernard Schleifer and Michael Hornburg for their elegant design work;

Pat Connolly, our dear firend, for contributing quotations, her delightful poem, photos of her children, Liam and Sara, and her loving encouragement throughout the entire process;

Eleanor Rielander, whose amazing talent with gum paste flowers inspired us both, as well as all other sugar artists whose books have been so helpful;

Dee Dalquist, editor of "Mailbox News," for being the first to share our work with cake enthusiasts all over the world;

Pilar and Musa Kurdi, for turning our designs into precise and handy flower cutters;

Mike's Lumber of Manhattan's Upper West Side, for cake boards that always gave support;

Frances Picone, who generously introduced us to the benevolent overseer of the Culture Courses at New York's Nippon Club, Naoko Yaegashi;

Every one of our students, who have taught us so much in return;

All of our cake clients, especially thoses who gave us creative freedom;

Paula Roberts, the English psychic, whose extraordinary talent brought us clarity and comfort;

Pamela Lincoln, our former acting teacher, who taught us how to express all our emotional colors;

My brother, Stephen Woolley, as well as his wife Barbara, who exposed me to the wonder of Nature at an early age, and Nina Aimable, who taught me so much about love and laughter;

My mother, Delores Farace, a fabulous baker and cake decorator in her own right;

And Boo and Hellzee, our faithful feline friends, who kept us company and always cheered us up when we needed it most.

Thanks again to all. We couldn't have done it without you!

Introducing Myself

A CHERRY TREE FLOURISHED IN MY BACKYARD WHEN I WAS A CHILD in York, Pennsylvania. Every June, I'd pick a bucketful of ripe fruit for my mother's homemade pies, just before the birds finished them off. With flour, sugar, and a flick of her rolling pin, a delicious goody miraculously appeared from the oven. I wanted to try my hand at it, too! With Mother's guidance, I succeeded at making my first cherry pie and discovered a hobby that offered sweet rewards, with no idea that I'd found my future career.

My father, an inspiring voice teacher, led me to also develop my talent as a singer. In 1975, at the age of twenty, I moved to New York City to pursue a career in the performing arts. Like most singer/actors, I needed to supplement my income in between jobs. Baking desserts seemed a far more appealing way to earn extra money than bartending or waiting on tables. So, I became a free-lance baker, selling pies, cookies, and cakes to nearby shops and restaurants.

Soon, requests for decorated cakes encouraged me to expand my knowledge of the confectionery arts. I learned on my own simply by doing and with the help of books. Having no formal art training, I sometimes felt afraid to attempt more challenging designs. But following the example of my great-great-great-great grandfather, Daniel Boone, the American pioneer, I chose instead to break through the boundaries of fear to explore new frontiers in the world of cake decorating.

Juggling a cake business and an acting career, however, was diffi-cult. After years of only occasional work on the "soaps," I landed a role in a Gershwin musical. Ironically, it was entitled *Let 'em Eat Cake!* When the show was over, I decided to commit myself whole-heartedly to my career as a confectionery artist. At that point, too,

Michael Farace, my gifted partner in life, climbed aboard the enterprise, and decorated cakes took center stage for both of us.

To enhance the beauty of our wedding and floral cakes, we began to investigate the amazing art of gum paste flowers. With this medium, it was possible to produce an unlimited variety of lifelike sugar flowers. What a boon to decorating! Learning to form each flower is a meditation of shape and color, teaching so much about patience, perseverance, and the splendor of Mother Earth.

For several years, I have taught classes in the fine art of cake decorating to students from over twenty countries, with an emphasis on sugar flowers. I encourage beginners to relax, allow mistakes, and take the pressure off to succeed. Learning anything of value takes time. Be kind to yourself and trust that you will improve with practice. Avoid the trap of judging or comparing your work to anyone else's. Everyone is an artist no matter what level of expertise they have achieved. It's only fear that tells us we're not good enough. With time, your own individual style will blossom and unfold. You'll gaze at your creations with wonder and say, "Wow! Did I do that?"

Seventeen years of effort, exploration, and fun have gone into the making of this book. Most importantly, I've learned that working patiently, step-by-step, is the key to unlocking the imagination and an effective way to develop one's gifts and talents. With our book as your guide, may you find joy and delight creating your own flowers, cakes, and beyond.

Welcome to the world of *Cakes by Design*!

SCOTT CLARK WOOLLEY

A Partner in Art

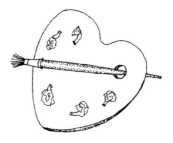

AS A CHILD, I WAS MESMERIZED BY PAINTINGS DONE BY MY OLDER cousin Sam. He turned paint and canvas into something wondrous to behold. I knew I wanted to make that kind of magic happen, too! But when I began art classes in school, I lost heart because of discouraging criticism from teachers and from an impatient voice inside my head expecting quick results. My dream of being a painter soon faded.

In high school I developed a passion for the performing arts, and after earning a bachelor's degree in theater, I moved to New York City to pursue an acting career. In order to make my proverbial ends meet, I moonlighted as a manager for one of the top caterers. That's where I met an ingenious cake decorator who had been hired to design a special effect for the thousandth performance of the Broadway hit *Evita*. Right away I wanted to lend a helping hand by locating a plaster bust of Eva Peron, enabling him to sculpt one in marzipan as the crowning touch atop his creation. It was the start of a partnership that would transform us both.

For the next few years, I watched the development of Scott's craftsmanship with cakes, offering ideas and assistance whenever I could. Getting only sporadic work as an actor on daytime television, I began to yearn for a career where I could express my creativity more often and also earn a living. What I was looking for was right there in front of me! So in 1987, I said good-bye to show business and enthusiastically became Scott's full-time partner in the artful world of cake decorating.

Since then, we've created hundreds of custom-order cakes and other works of sugar art for virtually every occasion under the sun. As collaborator, I get to play a wide variety of supporting roles. My favorite is painting glorious three-dimensional flowers. In a completely unexpected way, my childhood dream has come true. The palette and brushes are back in my hands again, only now my canvas is sugar! Turning simple dough into lifelike flowers is truly magical. And I've discovered that by taking the time to be true to Nature, my eyes are opened anew to the breathtaking wonders that abound in this magnificent garden called Earth.

Writing and compiling *Cakes by Design* has been yet another exciting opportunity to collaborate with Scott. It is my hope that our book encourages you to discover or rediscover the artist within you and inspires you to imagine endless possibilities.

Sweet dreams!

MICHAEL G. FARACE

PART ONE

❖ ❖ ❖

Baking and Decorating Techniques

Beginning

You can do this! The basic ingredients and equipment required can be found in most kitchens, so it's easy and inexpensive to start baking and decorating beautiful cakes. With very few special tools needed, one can embark on a delightful journey full of fun and imagination. So many of the important moments in life are celebrated with these sweet creations. How rewarding it is to make those moments more memorable with a one-of-a-kind decorated cake! And, personally handcrafting the decorations in sugar will touch hearts even more deeply.

Part One provides an introduction to baking cakes, recipes, as well as various sugar techniques for decorating. All the creations in this book were made using these easy methods. May the following help and inspire you as you explore the world of sugar art.

"Whatever you can do or dream you can,
Begin it!
Boldness has genius, power, magic in it!"
JOHANN WOLFGANG VON GOETHE

Basic Equipment

HEAVY-DUTY MIXER

A strong upright mixer is essential for most baking and decorating needs. Handheld types will overheat. I prefer a 6-quart KitchenAid mixer model KSM5.

SPATULAS

Rubber spatulas to scrape bowls cleanly; metal ones to spread icings smoothly.

CAKE PANS

Sturdy baking pans at least 1½" (4cm) deep, available in many shapes and sizes.

CAKE BOARDS

Inflexible surfaces for presentation (cardboard, wood, Lucite, etc.). I prefer ½" (1cm) particle boards wrapped with foil paper or covered with flowed sugar or fondant.

TURNTABLE

Revolving cake stand for easier frosting and decorating.

PIPING BAGS

Plastic-coated canvas bags with attachable couplers, making interchange of decorating tips easy.

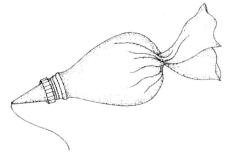

DECORATING TIPS

Various nozzles that are attached to piping bags for creating different effects with icing.

Hints on Baking

A BEAUTIFULLY DECORATED CAKE CAN TASTE AS GOOD AS IT LOOKS.
True success always begins with the inside. The following are nine of
my favorite recipes, developed over the past seventeen years. I love
a dense layer cake with a thin spread of whipped icing between
the layers. These cakes are sturdy enough for cake sculptures and
extensive decorating. They stay moist and delicious up to a week
even at room temperature.

I've found that these cakes bake evenly and brown nicely in a
low oven at 300°F (150°C). It does take longer but the cake bakes
flatter with moister edges. Also, removing it from the oven at exactly
the right moment is less crucial, so you'll never burn a cake. If you're
using an electric oven, which tends to be hotter than gas or convec-
tion ovens, reduce the temperature to as low as 275°F (135°C).

Each recipe fills two 10" or 11" (26cm) round pans and serves
20 to 25. For easy removal from pans, lightly grease with white
shortening and dust with flour. Fill pans with batter up to 1-1½"
(3cm) deep. Raise oven shelves as high as possible and place pans in
middle of rack away from oven walls. If more than one shelf is being
used, switch pans once while baking. Most of these recipes take at
least an hour to bake. To determine when cake is fully done, press
finger lightly in center. It should be firm to the touch.

After removing from oven, run a knife around edge and let cool
for 5 minutes. Cover with plastic wrap, then place cutting board or
cookie sheet on top and flip over. Lift pan slowly as cake releases.
Fold plastic wrap up and over cake, sealing completely. Many a cake
has become dry by cooling on an open rack where it loses moisture.
Let cool and then place on level shelf in freezer. Filling and frosting
cakes directly from the freezer keeps crumbing to a minimum and
makes sculpting much easier.

Over the years, these cakes have received rave reviews from
clients as well as their guests. And, simply by varying the fillings, I've
been able to satisfy many different sweet desires. Happy Baking!

Banana Walnut Cake

For strict vegetarians like us or those who are allergic to dairy foods, this eggless and milkless recipe is a healthy and delicious alternative. Bananas add rich flavor and moistness to this light and chewy dessert. People go nuts and bananas for it!

Preheat oven to 300°F (150°C, gas mark 2).
Cream together until light:

> 1   *cup (225g/8oz) margarine*
> 1¹/₂   *cups raw or refined sugar*
>   *(300g/10¹/₂ oz demarara or caster sugar)*

Beat in:

> 1¹/₂   *cups (340g/12oz) mashed ripe bananas*

Add:

> 1   *teaspoon grated lemon zest*
> 2   *tablespoons fresh lemon juice*

Separately, mix dry ingredients:

> 4   *cups white or whole wheat flour*
>   *(500g/1lb 2oz plain white or wholemeal flour)*
> 2   *teaspoons baking soda (bicarbonate of soda)*
> ¹/₂   *teaspoon salt*

Add to creamed mixture in 3 parts alternating with:

> 1   *cup (240ml/8fl oz) water or soy milk*

End with dry ingredients.
Pour into pans and bake for about 1 hour.
Filling: Creamy Vanilla or Chocolate Icing

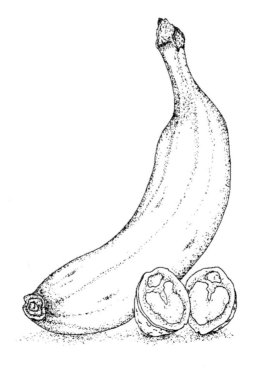

Carrot Raisin Walnut Cake

An abundant use of freshly grated carrots moistens this spicy crowd pleaser. Use a lighter oil, such as canola (rapeseed), safflower, or sunflower for this oil-based recipe. Delectable alone or spread with a thin layer of orange icing. I have a hunch you'll munch a bunch!

Preheat oven to 300°F (150°C, gas mark 2).

Grate:

- $^3/_4$ **pound raw carrots**

Place dry ingredients in mixer bowl and stir evenly:

- 2 **cups flour (250g/9oz plain flour)**
- $1^3/_4$ **cups sugar (350g/12$^1/_2$oz caster sugar)**
- 1 **teaspoon ground nutmeg**
- 2 **teaspoons ground cinnamon**
- 2 **teaspoons baking powder**
- 1 **teaspoon baking soda (bicarbonate of soda)**
- 1 **teaspoon salt**

Turn off mixer. Add:

- 4 **large eggs (size–3 eggs)**
- $1^1/_2$ **cups (360ml/12fl oz) vegetable oil**
- $^1/_2$ **the grated carrots**
- 1 **cup (115g/4oz) walnuts (check for shells!)**
- 1 **cup raisins (150g/5$^1/_2$ oz seedless raisins)**

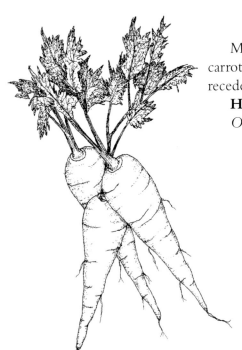

Mix at low speed, then beat for 2 minutes. Fold in remaining carrots. Pour into pans and bake for about 1 hour or until cake recedes from pan and is firm to the touch.

Hint: Careful not to jiggle while baking or cake will fall.

Other filling: Creamy Vanilla Icing

English Fruit Cake

In many countries, like Great Britain, fruit cake is the traditional choice for the wedding cake. Soaked in brandy and stored in a tin for months, or even years, it is then topped with marzipan and covered with royal icing. In America, commercially made fruit cakes are notorious for being dry and inedible. Try this recipe for a tasty holiday treat that no one will turn down.

Preheat oven to 300°F (150°C, gas mark 2).

Cream together until light:

   1   *cup (225g/8oz) unsalted butter or margarine*
   2   *cups brown sugar (400g/14oz soft brown sugar)*

Beat in, one at a time:

   4   *large eggs (size-3 eggs)*

Add:

   2   *tablespoons molasses*
   1   *teaspoon vanilla extract (vanilla essence)*

In separate bowl, stir together:

   2   *cups flour (250g/9oz plain flour)*
   1   *teaspoon ground allspice*
   1   *teaspoon ground cinnamon*
   1   *teaspoon ground ginger*
   $^{1}/_{2}$ *teaspoon ground cloves*
   $^{1}/_{2}$ *teaspoon ground nutmeg*

Mix into creamed sugar. Add:

   2   *tablespoons brandy*
   $^{1}/_{4}$ *cup (30g/1oz) blanched almonds*
   1   *cup (115g/4oz) pecans*
   1   *cup raisins (150g/5$^{1}/_{2}$oz seedless rainins)*
   1   *cup golden raisins (150g/5$^{1}/_{2}$oz sultanas)*
   1   *cup (150g/5$^{1}/_{2}$oz) currants*
   $^{1}/_{2}$ *cup candied cherries (85g/3oz glacé cherries)*
   $^{1}/_{2}$ *cup (85g/3oz) chopped candied citrus peel*

Pour into one 10" (26cm) round or bread loaf pan and bake for about 1 hour.

When done, run knife around sides and flip onto wire rack to cool.

Drizzle with brandy and wrap in brandy-soaked dish towel (tea towel) in a tightly sealed container. Keep in a cool place for storage and occasionally resoak with brandy. This is one cake that improves with age.

Fudge Brownie Cake

Rich and dense like a brownie, this cake will satisfy even the most demanding choco-holic. Or omit the nuts for a simply luscious chocolate indulgence.

Preheat oven to 300°F (150°C, gas mark 2).
Place dry ingredients in mixer bowl and stir evenly:

- 1½ cups (135g/scant 5oz) *unsweetened cocoa powder*
- 3 cups flour (375g/13oz *plain flour*)
- 2 cups sugar (400g/14oz *caster sugar*)
- ·1½ teaspoons baking soda (*bicarbonate of soda*)
- 1 teaspoon salt

Add all at once and stir to mix:

- 3 large eggs (*size-3 eggs*)
- 1 cup buttermilk (240ml/8fl oz)
- ¾ cup (170g/6oz) unsalted butter or margarine
- ⅔ cup (150ml/ ¼ pint) vegetable oil
- 2 teaspoons vanilla extract (*vanilla essence*)

Beat for 2 minutes, scraping bowl once. Stir in:

- 1½ cups (360ml/12fl oz) boiling water or coffee
- 1 cup (115g/4oz) chopped nuts
  (*walnuts, roasted almonds, or hazelnuts*)

Pour into pans and bake for about 1 hour.
Fillings: Chocolate, Vanilla, Mocha, Mint, or Coffee Icing

Golden Vanilla Cake

Lighter than a pound cake yet similar in richness, this yellow cake is a popular choice for weddings. Its subtle flavor complements any menu. With a hint of lemon to cleanse the palate, it is simply delicious.

Preheat oven to 300°F (150°C, gas mark 2).
Cream together until light:

1	cup (225g/8oz) unsalted butter or margarine
1³/₄	cups sugar (350g/12¹/₂ oz caster sugar)

Beat in, one at a time:

4	large eggs (size-3 eggs)

Add:

1	teaspoon grated lemon zest
1¹/₂	teaspoons vanilla extract (vanilla essence)

In separate bowl, mix:

3	cups flour (375g/13oz plain flour)
¹/₂	teaspoon salt
3	teaspoons baking powder

Add to creamed sugar in 3 parts alternating with:

1	cup (240ml/8fl oz) buttermilk

Pour into prepared pans and bake for about 1 hour.
Fillings: Creamy Vanilla, Lemon, or Chocolate Icing

Poppy Seed Cake

Divinely subtle in flavor, this white vanilla cake dotted with black poppy seeds is light and pleasing. A unique choice for weddings, it's lovely on a plate and goes well with fresh fruit or any sorbet. Tasteful in every way!

In a cup of water, soak for 2 hours:

½ cup (85g/3oz) poppy seeds

Preheat oven to 300°F (150°C, gas mark 2).
Cream together until light:

1 cup (225g/8oz) unsalted butter or margarine
1¾ cups sugar (350g/12½oz caster sugar)

Add drained poppy seeds and:

1½ teaspoons vanilla extract (vanilla essence)

Separately, mix dry ingredients:

3 cups flour (375g/13oz plain flour)
3 teaspoons baking powder
½ teaspoon salt

Alternate adding dry mixture and:

1 cup (240ml/8fl oz) water or milk

To creamed sugar. End with dry ingredients.
Beat:

4 egg whites

Until stiff peaks form and fold into batter.
Pour into pans and bake for about 1 hour.
Filling: Creamy Vanilla Icing

Roasted Hazelnut Cake

The enticing aroma of roasting hazelnuts makes this one of my favorite cakes to bake and its scrumptious flavor always has clients asking for more. Adding beaten egg whites to the speckled batter gives it a delicate texture. Delightful even without filling. Mmmmmmm.

PREPARING NUTS

Preheat oven to 425°F (220°C, gas mark 7).

Place ¼ pound (115g) hazelnuts or filberts on baking sheet and roast for 13-15 minutes. Do not burn. Let cool. To remove skins, rub between palms. Grind finely in food processor.

Lower oven to 300°F (150°C, gas mark 2).
Cream together until light:

> 1 *cup (225g/8oz) unsalted butter or margarine*
> 1³/4 *cups sugar (350g/12¹/2oz caster sugar)*

Beat in:

> 4 *large egg yolks (size-3 egg yolks)*

Add:

> 1 *cup (85g/3oz) ground nuts*

In separate bowl, mix together:

> 2 *cups flour (280g/9oz plain flour)*
> 2 *teaspoons baking powder*
> ¹/2 *teaspoon salt*

Alternate adding dry ingredients and:

> 1 *cup (240ml/8fl oz) buttermilk*

To the creamed sugar. End with dry ingredients.
In separate bowl, beat stiffly:

> 4 *egg whites*

Fold into batter. Pour into pans and bake for about 1 hour.
Fillings: Mocha, Coffee, or Creamy Vanilla Icing

Sour Cream Spice Cake

This rich and flavorful cake is especially nice in the fall and winter months. Use the freshest spices available, mostly found in health food stores. Commercially packaged spices are often stale and flavorless. For a tempting treat, spread lemon icing thinly between the layers. Yummy!

Preheat oven to 300°F (150°C, gas mark 2).
Cream together until light:

$1^3/_4$ *cups sugar (350g/12$^1/_2$oz caster sugar)*
1   *cup (225g/8oz) unsalted butter or margarine*

Beat in, one at a time:

4   *large eggs (size-3 eggs)*

And stir in:

1   *cup (240ml/8 fl oz) sour cream*

Separately, mix dry ingredients:

$3^1/_4$ *cups flour (400g/14oz plain flour)*
2   *teaspoons baking powder*
1   *teaspoon ground cinnamon*
1   *teaspoon ground nutmeg*
1   *teaspoon ground cloves*
$^1/_2$ *teaspoon salt*

Combine:

1   *teaspoon baking soda (bicarbonate of soda)*
$^1/_2$ *cup (120ml/4fl oz) hot water*

Stir half of dry mixture into creamed sugar followed by soda water.
Then add remaining dry ingredients and mix evenly.
Pour into pans and bake for about 1 hour.
Other filling: Creamy Vanilla Icing

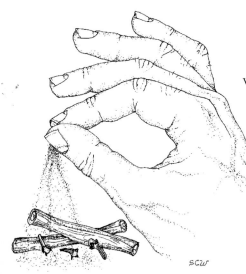

SCW

Zesty Lemon Cake

Another favorite for wedding cakes, this blend of sweet and sour tingles the tastebuds. A generous amount of freshly grated lemon rind or zest flecks this moist yellow cake. Mouthwatering served cold. So, pucker up!

Preheat oven to 300°F (150°C, gas mark 2).
Cream together until light:

  1 *cup (225g/8oz) unsalted butter or margarine*
  2 *cups sugar (400g/14oz caster sugar)*

Beat in, one at a time:

  4 *large eggs (size-3 eggs)*
  ½ *teaspoon salt*
     finely grated zest of 2 lemons

Alternate adding:

  3 *cups flour (375g/13oz plain flour)*
  1 *teaspoon baking soda (bicarbonate of soda)*
  2 *teaspoons baking powder*

And:

  1 *cup (240ml/8floz) buttermilk*

To creamed sugar. End with dry ingredients.
Mix in evenly:

  ⅓ *cup (80ml/scant 3fl oz) fresh lemon juice*
     (about 3 lemons)

Pour into pans and bake for about 1 hour.
Fillings: Lemon or Creamy Vanilla Icing

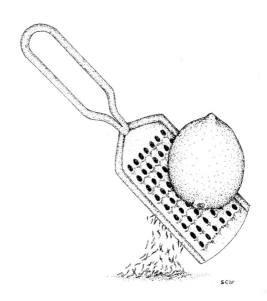

White Vanilla Icing

This sturdy snow-white icing is used for filling, decorating, and covering the outside of cakes. The high melting point of the shortening allows decorated cakes to remain unchanged in warm temperatures, perfect for those outdoor summer weddings. It will last for weeks when refrigerated. Rebeat to regain original consistency.

Place in mixer bowl:

2½	*cups white shortening (565g/1¼lb white vegetable fat)*
4	*tablespoons water*
2 to 3	*teaspoons clear vanilla extract (vanilla essence)*
½	*teaspoon salt*

Beat in slowly:

6	*cups confectioners' sugar (720g/1lb10oz icing sugar)*

Alternate adding:

4	*tablespoons water*
6	*cups confectioners' sugar (720g/1lb10oz icing sugar)*

Beat to whip.

Yield: 12 cups. Covers a 12" x 16" (30 x 40cm) sheet cake or 16" (40cm) round.

Hint: To determine proper consistency, turn mixer off. Icing should be stiff and hardly move. If not, add more sugar. For filling or decorating purposes, add a few drops of water to slightly loosen icing.

Creamy Vanilla Icing

Follow above recipe but substitute unsalted butter or margarine for white shortening (vegetable fat) and use regular vanilla extract (vanilla essence).

Chocolate Icing

Place 1¼ cups (115g/4oz) cocoa powder in small bowl and stir in 6 tablespoons vegetable oil to liquefy. Add to prepared vanilla icing. Beat until mixed evenly.

Coffee Icing

Dissolve 2 tablespoons instant coffee in 4 tablespoons boiling water. Let cool. Prepare vanilla icing and substitute coffee for 4 tablespoons water.

Mocha Icing

Liquefy ¾ cup (70g/2½oz) cocoa powder with 3 tablespoons vegetable oil and beat into coffee icing.

Lemon Icing

Prepare vanilla icing and add grated zest of 2 lemons. Substitute fresh juice for water.

Orange Icing

Prepare vanilla icing and add 3-4 teaspoons grated orange zest. Substitute orange juice for water.

Mint Icing

Prepare vanilla icing and add 2-3 teaspoons peppermint or spearmint extract.

Frosting the Cake

"Don't fight forces—use them."
BUCKMINSTER FULLER

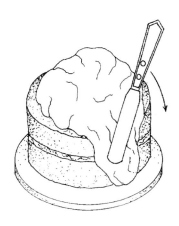

Spread icing thinly on center of cake board. Remove filled cake from freezer and place on top. Cover top of cake with large mound of icing. Spread over side with 6" (15cm) straight metal spatula (palette knife). Continue around cake working icing down over the sides. Scrape off excess.

To smooth icing, from this point on, use a hot spatula. Dip blade into boiling water, dry with paper towel and quickly run along sides while spinning turntable. With a bent 8" (20cm) spatula, smooth top by scraping outside edge to the center.

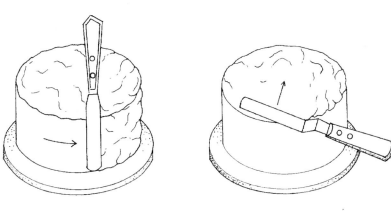

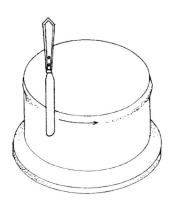

Finally, run 4" (10cm) spatula around upper edge to straighten sides completely.

Rolled Fondant

The beautifully smooth texture of this icing makes an elegant covering for cakes. Its sturdy nature allows them to be kept at room temperature for days without change, giving the artist ample time for decorating. Mixed evenly with gum paste, it's a handy, slow-drying sugar dough for sculpting flowers and other decorations.

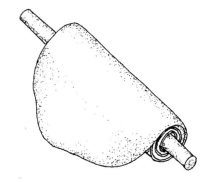

In small bowl, mix:

- **1**   *tablespoon unflavored gelatin*
- **4**   *tablespoons cool water*

Set in simmering saucepan to dissolve.
Melt in:

- **2**   *tablespoons white shortening (30g/1oz white vegetable fat)*

Then add:

- **1/2**   *cup (120ml/4floz) glucose (or white corn syrup)*
- **1**   *teaspoon clear vanilla extract (vanilla essence)*

Grease large bowl and fill with:

- **7**   *cups sifted confectioners' sugar (840g/1lb 14oz icing sugar)*

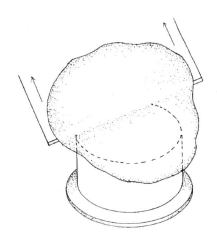

Make well in center of sugar bowl and pour in liquid mixture. Stir slowly to incorporate. Remove from bowl and knead on board dusted with confectioners' (icing) sugar until smooth. Cover with plastic wrap and set in an air-tight container at room temperature.

Hint: If using immediately, knead briefly on board dusted with cornstarch (cornflour) to stiffen.

For colored fondant, add food paste color to liquid before adding sugar. This recipe covers a high 9" (23cm) or 10" (26cm) cake and can last for months.

Covering Cake

Lightly dust smooth side of masonite board with confectioners' (icing) sugar. Roll out fondant to a ¼" (6mm) thickness, large enough to cover top and sides of cake. Prick any bubbles with pin and push out air with fingertips. Hold board above cake and slide fondant onto cake. Smooth top surface with fingertips, using circular motion. Gently smooth icing down sides with palms, removing any pleating. Cut off excess at bottom with circular blade.

Hint: If lacking masonite, roll icing around rolling pin to lift and lay onto cake.

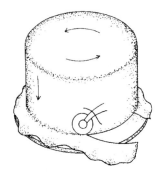

"IVORY HOUR"
A floribunda rose sculpted in sugar beautifies each tier of this elegant wedding cake covered with ivory fondant.

Stacking Cakes

Many of the creations in this book were constructed by stacking cakes on top of one another. With just cardboard and wooden dowels for support, quite grand structures like multitiered wedding cakes are possible. For large basket cakes, stacking forms a dramatic 8" (20cm) tall base with plenty of room for weaving.

METHOD

Place frozen filled cake on board and frost. Insert 6 narrow wooden dowels in circle and 1 in the middle. Snip off excess with heavy shears. Place circle of wax paper on top and spread with thin layer of icing.

To prepare second cake, place on same-size cardboard circle and frost. Lift carefully and place on first cake, centering carefully.

For 3 or more tiers, place dowels in every cake but top and use stronger dowels in bottom cake.

For tall baskets, stack 2 same-size cakes. Or, for graceful, sloping sides, prepare top cake 1" (3cm) wider than bottom and carve as shown.

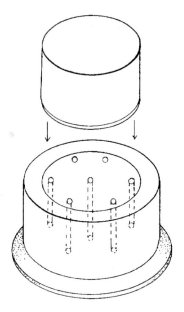

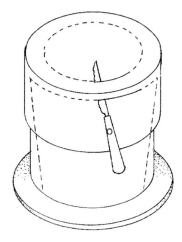

"SIMPLE & SWEET"

Stacking cakes allows for continuous movement of decoration and creates a sense of oneness. Tiny gum paste blossoms dance beneath miniature lilies, roses, sweet peas, and stephanotis.

Colonnades

For generations, tier separators of all kinds have raised the art of cake decorating to new heights never before imagined. These statuesque columns can transform the tiers of a cake into a towering masterpiece. Try making and decorating your own to match the style of your design, rather than relying on the commercially made plastic variety. The following is a simple method using sugar dough and wooden dowels to build a sturdy tier separator 5" (12cm) high with 3 round columns.

MATERIALS REQUIRED

Sugar Dough (an even mixture of fondant and gum paste)
3   **wooden dowels (⁵/₈" thick and 4¹/₂" long). (16mm x 11cm)**
2   **foam board circles (5" and 6" diameters) (12 and 16cm)**
6   **nails (³/₄" long with flat heads) (19mm)**
    hammer
    glue (for wood or paper)
    sturdy white paper
    ribbon (¹/₄" wide) (7mm)

PILLARS

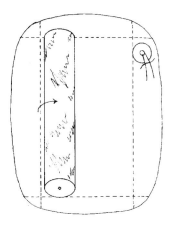

To cover dowels, roll out dough moderately thick and turn over. Brush dowel with gum glue and set on left of dough. With circular blade, cut straight edge on left, top, and bottom. Then roll dowel to cover, cutting off excess on right side. Let dry standing overnight.

Hint: Once dry, press bits of dough into seam and then smooth with fine sandpaper.

Optional: For ribbed columns, press parallel lines into dough with edge of ruler before covering dowel.

Handcrafted tier separators add a look of individuality and show loving attention to detail.

"LOVE OVERFLOWING"
For a traditional look, put the bridal cake on a pedestal with pillars sculpted in sugar. Here, hard sugar leaves embellish soft piped flowers.

TOP AND BOTTOM

Divide 5" (12cm) circle into thirds like a pie. (If a compass is handy, mark lines at 0°, 120°, and 240°.) Mark a dot 2" (5cm) from the center on each line. Then place in center of 6" (15cm) circle and poke needle tool through dots to mark holes for nails. To keep dots in alignment, circle one dot top and bottom as a reminder.

To cover bottom, roll out dough moderately thick. Brush 6" (15cm) circle with gum glue and cover with dough. Cut along edge with circular blade to remove excess. Poke needle tool up through holes. Let dry.

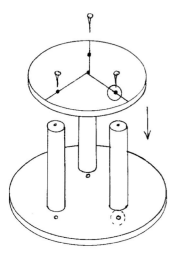

ASSEMBLY

Insert a nail into any hole in 5" (12cm) circle. Dab wood glue on end of dowel and hammer nail into center. Repeat for other two. Set upside down and repeat process for bottom. Make sure circled dots share same pillar. Glue a circle of paper on top to hide nails and glue ribbon around edge. To finish pillars, roll tubes of various thicknesses of dough and attach to top and bottom of pillars with glue.

ATTACHING TO CAKE

Insert at least 5 thin dowels or skewers into lower cake to support tier separator. Spread a thin layer of royal icing in center and place separator on top. Pipe border around bottom edge to secure. Spread icing on top to attach upper tier securely.

VARIATIONS

Adjusting the number, height, and thickness of the dowels can alter the look of your handcrafted colonnade. Square and rectangular dowels work well for cakes with corners.

For a faster construction, wrap dowels and bottom with glossy paper or gold or silver foil. Simply tape strip of paper to dowel and roll to cover, securing end with glue. Once dry, a moist paper towel will clean up excess glue. Wrap base to match cake board.

Decorative ideas: To marbleize pillars, mix 2 or 3 shades of dough unevenly before rolling out. For a romantic touch, pipe a spiral vine up pillar with royal icing and attach tiny gum paste leaves.

Basket Cakes

Ah! What could be more breathtaking than a beautiful basket of flowers, especially when the basket is a cake and the flowers are made of sugar. The arts of cake decorating and basket weaving are combined uniquely to create wondrous illusions. Many basket-weave patterns are easily simulated with a piping bag and icing.

BASIC WEAVE

Frost cake thinly with icing. With ruler, mark vertical lines around cake at ¾"(19mm) intervals. Because 2 different decorating tips are used for this pattern, fill 2 bags with icing to avoid switching tips. Using #8 or #9 tip, pipe a vertical "cord" from top to bottom. With #45 tip, pipe horizontal ribbons over cord. Each ribbon should stretch from the mark left of cord to one on the right. Make sure space between ribbons is slightly wider than the width of ribbon.

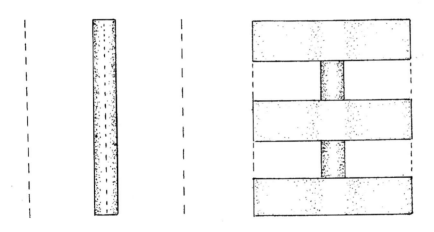

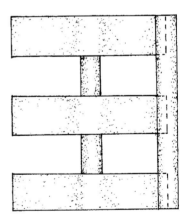

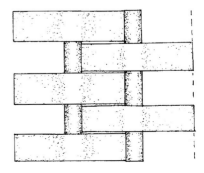

Pipe another vertical cord over next mark covering the ends of ribbons. Tuck ribbon tip under first cord, pipe and stretch ribbon over second, ending at next vertical mark. Continue on switching between cords and ribbons to finish basket weave.

Hint: An even number of vertical lines around cake will finish basket weave neatly.

VARIATIONS

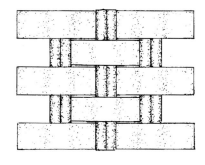

DOUBLE CORD: Pipe 2 vertical lines next to each other, using any tip #7-10, then pipe horizontal ribbons with tip #45.

WICKER: Pipe vertical and horizontal lines using any tip #7-10. Adjust tightness of weave by increasing or decreasing distance between verticals.

PICNIC BASKET: Pipe vertical and horizontal lines with ribbon tip #45.

"A MONARCH'S DELIGHT"
Chocolate and mocha icings were interwoven for this basket of spring flowers that attracted the attention of a monarch butterfly.

"A TISKET, A TASKET"
Twisted twigs bind a rustic basket cake, dripping with lilacs piped in soft icing.

OTHER PATTERNS

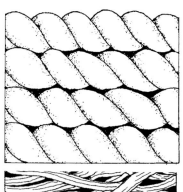

ROPE BASKET: Begin at base of cake and pipe rings of rope borders on top of one another, using tip #9 or #10. Mark horizontal lines on cake as a guide to keep rings level.
Suggestion: A single line of rope pattern is an excellent top or bottom border for most basket weaves.

TWIST O' TWIGS: Very simple to do. Using any tips #4-9, pipe uneven horizontal lines around cake, overlapping freely until entire area is covered.

PUSSY WILLOW BUNDLE: Prepare catkins on toothpicks as for Pussy Willow. Pipe vertical or horizontal branches in chocolate or brown icing. Insert catkins at irregular intervals.

"UNHAMPERED BEAUTIES"
Sugar rings and a band painted gold enhance a double-decker rope basket bulging with roses.

"TULIPS AND WILLOWS"
Sugar catkins dot chocolate branches to form a delightful pussy willow basket of vibrant tulips. A white cabbage butterfly adds a bit of whimsy.

What is Royal Icing?

Despite its fancy name, this versatile decorating icing is simple to make. Royal icing is a whipped mixture of egg whites, confectioners' icing sugar, and cream of tartar that dries completely hard and crisp. Finer than other icings, it is excellent for piping precise sugar decorations, such as stringwork, lattices, and lace points. When liquefied, it can be flowed within a piped outline and allowed to dry to form strong, thick sugar pieces. This technique, known as floodwork or run sugar, is indispensable when copying lettering, logos, or reproducing artwork. And, pieces can be made well in advance to make last-minute decorating easier.

Royal Icing

Place in mixer bowl:

> 2 *extra large egg whites (size-1 egg whites) at room temperature*
> 1/4 *teaspoon cream of tartar*

Beat in gradually:

2¹/₂-3 cups confectioners' sugar (300-360/10¹/₂-12oz icing sugar

Add enough sugar to form soft peaks.
Whip at high speed for at least 3 minutes.
Icing should be slightly glossy in appearance. It dries quickly when exposed to air, so keep bowl covered.
Hint: Meringue powder and water can be substituted for egg whites.

"FLOWERS AND FILIGREE"
Royal icing lattice, lace points, and scrolls cascade down this Victorian-style wedding cake. Lilies, roses, and tiny mums bedeck each tier.

Lattices

Similar to a garden trellis, this open framework of sugar makes a dazzling top for a wedding cake. Three or more flat pieces are joined to form an intricate structure, creating an amazing backdrop for flowers. Look at what a few lines and dots of royal icing can do!

Make 2 copies of pattern and tape to flat surface covered with wax paper. With tip #3 or #4, pipe "L" shape first, then curved lines followed by dots. Make 3 for round cakes and 4 for square. Let dry at least 6 hours. Remove tape and carefully peel off wax paper.

To assemble, run a line of royal icing along straight edge of left pattern and stand on cake. Connect vertical side of right pattern and set angle. Pipe dots at base to secure. Add third or fourth side similarly. Lattice may be assembled separately on wax paper and then carefully placed on cake.

Close-up of lattice work.

Floodwork

Many of the unique sugar decorations created for the cakes in this book were made using this simple technique. When dry, the smooth flat surface of floodwork becomes a wonderful canvas, allowing the artist to paint with great detail. Unpainted pieces have a marvelously precise look as well. Learning this helpful method is simply invaluable.

SET UP

To copy any image, first tape it to a flat, inflexible surface. Make sure there are no ripples by taping all corners and sides. Cover with wax paper and tape tightly over art.

Prepare recipe of royal icing and reserve at least ½ cup (120ml) for piping outlines. Place remainder in medium bowl and slowly stir in water until icing liquefies. To check for proper consistency, drizzle a spoonful of icing back into bowl. If line of icing takes longer than 3 seconds to vanish, mixture is too thick. Add a few drops of water and check again. Let sit 10-15 minutes, allowing bubbles to rise to surface. Sweep a paintbrush across top to pop bubbles.

OUTLINING

The color of icing used to pipe outlines can make a difference. Generally use the same color as the piece being flowed. Just add a touch of food paste color with a toothpick to the reserved royal icing and place in piping bag. Use tip #1 for lettering and delicate shapes and #2 or #3 for larger pieces. When outlining, make sure all corners are closed to hold in the liquefied sugar about to be flowed. Let outline dry 5 minutes before flowing.

Hint: Pipe outline in white for multicolored pieces.

FLOWING SUGAR

Before flowing, stir in another ¼ teaspoon cream of tartar to liquefied sugar to speed drying. Most flowed sugar takes 24 hours to dry, larger pieces as long as 48 hours.

Using brushes to flow sugar within piped outlines lends control and precision to this process. To begin, dip a small rounded paintbrush into icing, halfway up metal band. Lift and roll handle between fingers to keep icing from dripping. Move to area being flowed. Allow icing to run down brush filling in section. Tease edges of liquid to the piped outline with bristles. For adjacent sections, flow one

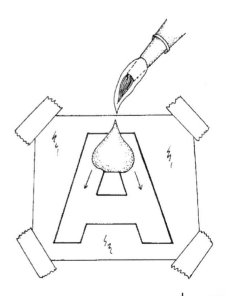

area and allow to dry until glossiness disappears. Then it is ready for neighboring area to be filled in. Immediately pop any bubbles with a toothpick. For larger sections, use larger brush or pour icing from spouted measuring cup. Be careful not to overflow outline.

Hint: When working more than an hour with floodwork, cream of tartar breaks down and is not as effective. Add a pinch or two to maintain its hardening effect.

COLORING FLOODWORK

Food paste colors intensify greatly during drying, so flow a lighter shade than you ultimately wish to achieve. Keep in mind that adding large amounts of color to flow will make the piece more fragile. To paint floodwork, use a brush to apply paste colors loosened with water. Be aware that sugar will dissolve if brush is too wet.

AFTER DRYING

Untape wax paper and carefully turn flowed sugar upside down on paper towel. Gingerly peel off wax paper. Attach floodwork to cake with dots of royal icing. Or, leave wax paper on and run exacto knife around edge to remove excess, if you wish to preserve the work.

"BABY'S BLOCKS"
The ABC's on this baby shower cake are easy to spell out using floodwork techniques.

First make sure that you have the best photograph available of the person you wish to capture, the larger the better. If necessary, make an enlargement.

Prepare image with wax paper as before. With #1 tip, pipe outlines of eyes, mouth, face, ears, hair, and neck. If teeth are showing, flow lips and open mouth as one.

For color portrait, first flow eyes and mouth white. Then flow face, ears, and neck with appropriate skin tone, followed by hair. If hairstyle is wavy or curly, outline sections and flow separately. Let dry at least 24 hours.

Place board with sugar piece on easel or slanted tabletop for easier painting. To paint the fine details of the face, use a 000 brush, water, and a palette of food paste colors. Paint eyes first followed by lips and teeth. Estimate the position of the nose. Then shade cheekbones, ears, and neck and paint hair last.

Hint: For a black-and-white portrait, simply flow sections in white and shades of gray. When painting, use black only for details and creating shadows.

"BLAST OFF!"
Boldly explore new worlds! Here, black royal icing was flowed directly onto a frosted cake and allowed to dry before adding stars, lettering, and painted floodwork decorations.

"PEANUT GALLERY"
A birthday cake for a sports nut, this stack of trading cards featured a portrait painted on floodwork. Oversize nuts and shells shaped in sugar dough scatter the board.

An easier and exciting way of presenting an image on cakes is through the use of silhouettes. A person or object can be uniquely suggested by capturing its specific outline. Pipe the outline and flow with the same color. For the classic silhouette, pipe outline black and flow with black icing. Or, choose any desired color that strongly contrasts the background.

"THE MAESTRO'S SCORE"
Silhouettes or unpainted floodwork can be overpiped with royal icing to add details and dimension.

*"Around the corner there may wait
A new road or a secret gate."*
J.R.R. TOLKIEN

What is Gum Paste?

There are many types of sugar doughs used for decorating, one of which is called "gum paste." The addition of powdered vegetable gum to the dough produces a substance that performs with great elasticity and also allows it to be rolled out paper thin without tearing. It is an excellent medium for creating an unlimited range of decorations, including lifelike flowers, creatures of the wild, ribbons, plaques and cards, just to name a few. Gum paste is hand worked at room temperature and, once exposed to the air, dries quickly to a hard and crisp texture. It may be painted with edible colors to exacting detail on its very smooth surface. These works of sugar art, if stored carefully or kept under glass or Lucite, will last for years. Like "Play-Doh," painting and sculpting this sugar dough is an enjoyable and rewarding experience for children of all ages.

Gum Paste

This easy gum paste recipe can be made by hand or by using a strong mixer, such as a KitchenAid. Weaker models or handheld mixers will burn out if used to beat this stiff dough. I recommend the mixer method, which whitens the dough and is simply less work. Both methods, however, will produce splendid results.

The finest quality vegetable gum to use is gum tragacanth and is available at most cake decorating stores. It may also be found in many pharmacies, since it is commonly used as a laxative. Premade gum paste mixes that simply require the addition of water are also available. To save time and effort, these provide another alternative.

Making gum paste is not an exact science. More or less of any one ingredient will still produce a usable dough. Experimentation with these proportions will lead you to find the texture you enjoy working with most. For flower making, I slightly reduce the confectioners' sugar for a moister dough, which gives a softer look to the petals. If a sharp, crisp look is desired for such things as place cards, mix a firmer dough by adding more sugar.

Place 1" (2.5cm) water in broad pan to simmer on stove. Combine in greased mixer bowl:

> *6 cups confectioners' sugar (720g/1lb 10oz icing sugar)*
> *3 tablespoons vegetable gum such as gum arabic (level)*

Place bowl in pan to warm sugar mixture. Stir twice. Meanwhile, dissolve together in small bowl:

> *4 teaspoons unflavored gelatin (level)*
> *6 tablespoons cool water*

Remove bowl from pan and attach to mixer. Place bowl of gelatin mixture into pan. Heat until clear.
Add:

> *1 tablespoon liquid glucose or clear corn syrup*

Pour into mixer bowl, followed by:

> *2 extra large egg whites (size-1 whites), at room temperature*

Beat until blended. Then slowly add until mixture stiffens:

> *1 cup confectioners' sugar (120g/4¼oz icing sugar), more or less*

Beat again until mixture whitens, scraping sides of bowl once. Remove from bowl, divide in half and place each portion in middle of large piece of plastic wrap (cling film). Fold sides over, removing all air pockets. Place in refrigerator or freezer to cool and stiffen dough.

Hint: In warm or humid climates, add ¼ cup cornstarch (30g/1oz cornflour) and reduce confectioners' sugar.

Yield: 2½–3 pounds (1.1–1.35kg)

HAND METHOD

In a large open bowl, form a well in the warmed sugar and gum mixture. Pour in gelatin mixture. Partially stir hot liquid into sugar. Then add egg whites and stir until mixed. Remove from bowl and knead on surface dusted with final cup of sugar. Wrap in plastic as above.

FINAL STEP

When hard, remove dough from refrigerator or freezer and allow it to come to room temperature before using. Grease hands with white shortening. Knead a portion of dough with thumbs and forefingers to a smooth texture. Roll into ball and place in fresh piece of plastic wrap, twisting tightly to prevent exposure to air. Seal in a zippered bag and refrigerate. Dough will last for months in refrigerator if worked once every two weeks.

Now you're ready to create a masterpiece!

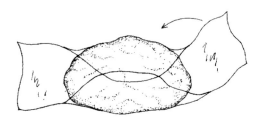

HANDY HINTS

To lengthen the drying time and allow for more leisurely sculpting, melt 1 tablespoon white shortening into gelatin mixture or work in by hand later.

If dough is too dry, dip into egg white or water and work in with greased fingertips. If too loose, work in cornstarch.

Since the varying grades of gum tragacanth can sometimes turn dough beige, a tiny drop of blue food paste color can be added to whiten sugar paste.

Standard Equipment

PLASTIC BOARD

Smooth, nonstick surface for rolling out dough. Plastic placemat may be substituted.

ROLLING PIN

Small plastic or wooden pin used to roll out dough.

FOAM PAD

Dense, firm pad (4" square/10cm) with smooth surface. Essential for thinning and ruffling edges. Back of placemat may be used.

BALL TOOL

Indispensable for thinning and ruffling edges on pad or in palm. Available in many sizes.

NEEDLE TOOL

Detail instrument for lining and marking sugar pieces.

CONE TOOL

Double-ended: smooth cone and umbrella shape. Use to hollow out and indent the centers of flowers.

FRILLER TOOL

Bent footed tool used to mash and frill edges for ruffling.

DOWEL

Round narrow stick used to create strong ruffles.

EXACTO KNIFE

Small razor blade tool used for cutting paste. Standard #11 suggested.

TWEEZERS

Bent nose variety is preferred for pinching dough, inserting stamens, etc.

TRACING WHEEL

Circular dressmaker's tool used to mark stitching on ribbons, etc.

PIZZA CUTTER

Circular blade used to cut shapes free-hand.

CUTTERS

Metal or plastic forms used to cut specific shapes from rolled out dough.

VEINERS

Texturing devices used to simulate veins in petals and leaves. Made of silicone, plastic, or ceramic.

FORMERS

Various molds used to shape dough when drying.

SCISSORS

Strong blades to cut wire; rounded cuticle scissors for detail work.

PAINTBRUSHES

Synthetic brushes used to apply wet and dry color to sugar pieces. (Animals needn't die for art.)

PIPING TIPS

Cake decorating tips used to sculpt details.

MUG

Low, widemouth heavy glass or mug used to build larger flowers.

Materials and Supplies

EGG WHITE

Used as an adhesive or glue. Substitute mixture of gum arabic and water, ratio 1:3.

WHITE SHORTENING

Used on board when rolling out and on hands to prevent sticking.

CORNSTARCH

Keeps tools from sticking to dough.

FOOD PASTE COLORS

For coloring dough and painting with wet brush.

PIPING GEL

Loosen with water and brush on dry pieces for a glossy effect.

PASTELS

Ground nontoxic chalks used to dust dry color onto sugar pieces. Commercially available as petal dust.

STAMENS

Stiff thread with tips for centers of flowers. Commercially available in many colors and sizes.

FLORAL WIRE

Cloth or paper-covered wire used to build and assemble flowers. Available in various thicknesses or gauges.

FLORAL TAPE

Gummy tape used to join wires and to form stems, tendrils, etc. Available in white, green, and brown.

TULLE

Fine mesh fabric used to texture dough.

TOOTHPICKS

Round wooden variety used for making tiny frills and ruffles.

PLASTIC WRAP

For storage and covering dough to prevent drying.

FIBER FILLING

Polyester or cotton used to lift and shape flowers and leaves.

STYROFOAM

Brittle plastic foam used to hold or stand wired sugar pieces for drying.

*"The mind learns by doing;
the heart learns by trying."*
Moonstone ("The Outer Limits")

Basic Techniques

AMOUNT OF DOUGH TO USE

Most novices tend to work with too much dough. To make it easier to select the appropriate amount, I have set the following standard sizes.

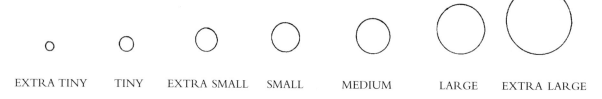

EXTRA TINY   TINY   EXTRA SMALL   SMALL   MEDIUM   LARGE   EXTRA LARGE

When sculpting, most pieces begin with a smooth ball. First work dough with greased fingertips. Lightly grease palm and roll dough with forefingers or palm of other hand into ball without creases. Then continue to sculpt desired shape.

When rolling out dough flat for cutting, pull more than enough to accommodate size of cutter.

ROLLING OUT

Lightly grease one side of board or placemat with white shortening and the other lightly dusted with cornstarch. Place dough on greased side and roll out with rolling pin to desired thickness.

Hint: Never flip dough after rolling out.

Pick up ends and slide over cornstarch area to coat back. This allows dough to maintain its shape and makes handling easier. Do not use too much or dough will dry too quickly. Now the dough is ready to be cut.

HOW THICK?

Thicknesses vary depending upon the subject being made. I have set the following standard thicknesses:

THIN: $\frac{1}{32}$" (1mm), translucent, rose petal thickness, will not hold wire.

MODERATELY THIN: $\frac{1}{16}$" (2mm), opaque, thick enough for most petals and leaves on 26–30g wires.

MODERATELY THICK: $\frac{3}{32}$" (3mm), for waxy petals and leaves on 22-24g wires.

THICK: $\frac{1}{8}$" (4mm), for structural pieces, plaques, ornaments, etc.

USING CUTTERS

Place cutter over dough on board lightly dusted with cornstarch. Press firmly and jiggle back and forth for a cleaner cut. Remove excess dough and save. Lift cutter. Use ball tool or paintbrush handle to poke out dough, should it remain inside cutter. A soft plastic placemat is particularly effective as a cutting surface as compared to a hard plastic board.

USING VEINERS

Every subject has a specific texture that can be achieved in many ways. Veiners produce lifelike impressions in the dough, simulating Nature's delicate lines on leaves and petals. Generally speaking, they are pressed onto soft dough *before* cutting out shape.

FORMING "HATS"

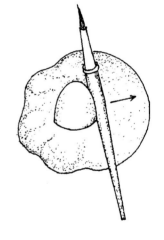

Molding dough into the shape of a hat is a common procedure when making many flowers and calyxes. With fingertips, form center mound shape. With index fingers and thumb, work out a brim. Place on lightly greased area. Using narrow paintbrush handle as shown, roll brim outward to thin. Place on cornstarch and cut. Make sure size of mound will fit inside cutter.

There are three basic hat shapes used:

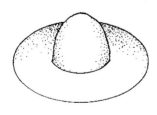

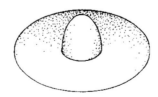

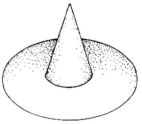

BOWLER

MEXICAN

WITCH

Using Pad

I recommend using a firm dense pad as a surface for thinning and ruffling edges. It's like having a third hand. It frees the hands to spin the sugar piece and work at the best angle. Before using, dust pad lightly with cornstarch. Never use grease or cut on pad. The primary tools used on the pad are the ball and needle tools.

Using Tools

BALL TOOL: Most work is done rolling this tool over edges of sugar on foam pad. Hold as shown, rather than like a pencil. Use large ball tool for most work. To thin edges, keep ball primarily on pad just catching side of dough. To ruffle, press firmly, roll and lift tool several times along edge. The smaller the ball tool, the smaller the ruffle. For soft movement, scoot around edge without rolling. Never grease this instrument. If sticking occurs, dip into cornstarch.

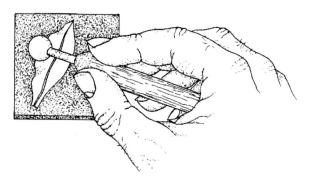

NEEDLE TOOL: Most detail work is done using the *side* of this instrument, not the point. Hold lightly with fingertips and thumb to create strong center veins, marking lines and pointing tips of petals. Also helpful when picking up sugar pieces. A hat pin or upholstery needle may be substituted.

CONE/UMBRELLA TOOL: The smooth cone is used for hollowing out dough and for pulled flowers; the umbrella end creates a starburst or pucker for flower centers and buds. Whenever using, dip end into cornstarch first.

FRILLER TOOL: Always grease this footed tool and surface area before mashing or distressing edges of dough. Hold like a pencil. Use on soft placemat for frilling.

Glue

To join sugar pieces, apply a minimal amount of egg white or gum arabic glue with an old detail brush. Too much dissolves dough and lengthens drying time. When inserting wires into soft dough, first dip into glue, then remove excess by pulling through folded crease in palm. Wires that are too wet create problems. Just damp is best.

Gum arabic glue is made with 1 part gum arabic to 3 parts water, shaken in a small jar. Let soak for 1 hour. This adhesive will dry somewhat slower than egg white but is nonperishable and can be kept at room temperature for months. Egg white needs to be refrigerated after use but will last up to a week.

General Rule: When joining pieces of wet and dry dough, always apply glue to the *wet* piece. They will stick together more easily that way.

Floral Wire

Working with cloth or paper-covered wires is a matter of personal preference. Since most flower stems are thick, I prefer the cloth type, except for the most delicate work. Cloth wires also take color more easily when dusted.

The sturdiness of the wire is determined by the gauge: the higher the number, the lighter the wire. I generally use 20 to 30 gauge. Choose the gauge according to the weight of the dough to be attached: 20-22 heavy, 24-26 medium, 28-30 light.

Before inserting into dough, the tips of wires are often formed into an eye hook in order to secure sugar piece. For heavier gauges, use needle-nose pliers to bend hook. When inserting an unhooked wire into a petal or leaf, hold base of sugar piece between index finger and thumb. Let your fingers tell you that the wire is within the dough, not protruding.

Note: When following these instructions, white wires are suggested, unless otherwise specified.

Floral Tape

This gummy tape is used to join wired sugar pieces and to form some delicate flower parts. For most wrapping, split tape into lengths ¼" (7mm) wide. Always stretch before using to expose its stickiness. Attach end of tape to wire with index finger and thumb, pinching firmly and spinning wire with other hand. Choice of color is again a matter of preference. I prefer white, which can then be dusted any specific color desired. For darker stem, use green. Floral tape may be purchased at florist supply and cake decorating stores.

In the following instructions, white tape is used unless otherwise stated.

DRYING TIMES

Generally speaking, dough rolled out at least moderately thin requires 12 to 24 hours at room temperature to dry completely. Pieces may crumble if handled too soon. The time may be drastically reduced by placing sugar pieces in a very low oven at 150°F. (66°C) or less for at least 2 hours. Certain smaller flowers, such as the sweet pea, may have their lightweight petals added after base has dried for only an hour or so. Thicker pieces and all flowers formed in mugs need at least 24 hours. All flower parts must be thoroughly dry before wrapping with floral tape.

COLORING DOUGH

Dip a toothpick into food paste color and apply to center of ball. Stretch and fold until color disperses evenly. Use shortening on fingertips when mixing. This will keep the color from dyeing hands.

Sugar dough lightens dramatically after drying. Color original dough a deeper shade than you wish to achieve. Most flowers have a light and translucent quality so a pastel base color is generally recommended. In the following instructions, dough is white unless otherwise specified.

DUSTING AND PAINTING

Color is also added to sugar pieces with dry and wet techniques. In these instructions, "dusting" refers to applying powdered color with a dry brush. This achieves a lifelike graduation of color, similar to airbrushing. Commercially made "petal dust" is available in a rainbow of colors and may be purchased at a cake decorating supplier. Nontoxic chalks or pastels, available at art supply stores, may be ground to a powder or simply shaved with an exacto knife. Simply add cornstarch to lighten vibrant colors to the desired shade.

"Painting" refers to applying food paste colors with a wet brush. Loosen pastes with a drop of water before use. Keep in mind that a brush that is too wet will dissolve sugar. This technique is excellent for creating sharp details, such as veins on butterflies and pansies, speckles on lilies and orchids, to name a few.

To bring sugar decorations to life, try at least three different colors in their creation. Even a white flower will appear more alive by adding yellow and green at the base of each petal. Use a touch of yellow whenever possible. The color of the sun adds life force to any flower. As a general rule, it's good to use two shades of the same color; the lighter one softens the hue and the darker adds depth and thins edges.

Hint: Gardening magazines are very helpful visual aids for painting sugar flowers and for coloring ideas.

BRUSH TECHNIQUES

Use a rounded end brush for all flat surfaces and hold like a pencil. For dusting, dip into color and brush lightly in one direction only. Do not scrub. As a general rule, travel in the direction of veins, beginning at base and moving outward. Use a flat brush for points and edges. Hold like a pencil with palm to the ceiling. Use side of brush to apply color. For painting fine details, use a 000 brush. As a rule, paint details with food paste color *after* dusting with dry color.

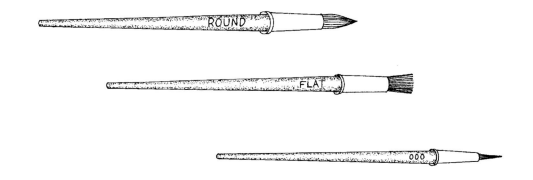

MIXING COLORS

The three primary colors are red, yellow, and blue. All other colors are achieved by mixing the neighboring primaries on the Color Wheel below in varying proportions. For instance, violet has red and blue as neighboring primaries, but being closer to red means that red is in greater proportion than blue. When mixing, begin with the lighter color and add the darker color gradually. Pastel shades on the outside circle of the wheel are achieved by adding white to the inner color.

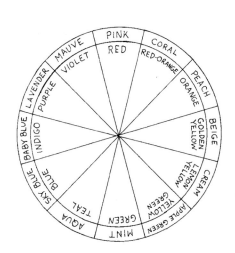

Textures

Always consider the specific textures of each subject. For a shiny look, brush with clear piping gel loosened with water and let dry for ½ hour. Brush most flowers lightly with "pearl dust" for a moist wet look as a finishing touch. Apply strongly on orchids, lilies, and tulips to approximate their waxy textures. For a powdery look, simply dust with dry colors. For "pollen" or a fuzzy appearance, brush with glue and sprinkle with a mixture of gelatin and dry pastel of the appropriate shade. Metallic effects are achieved by mixing nontoxic gold, silver, or bronze dust with vegetable oil or lemon extract to a thick consistency. These products are available at most cake decorating suppliers.

Guide to Symbols

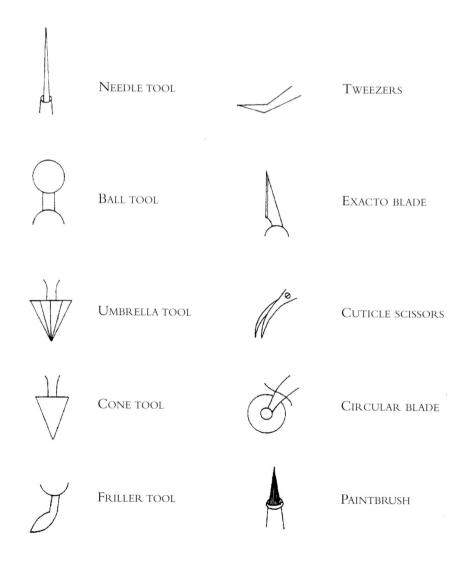

NEEDLE TOOL

TWEEZERS

BALL TOOL

EXACTO BLADE

UMBRELLA TOOL

CUTICLE SCISSORS

CONE TOOL

CIRCULAR BLADE

FRILLER TOOL

PAINTBRUSH

PART TWO

The Nature of Sugar Flowers

"I owe having become an artist to flowers."
CLAUDE MONET

To help discover the nature of sugar flowers, we have provided a step-by-step method for forming and painting each flower, along with diagrams and illustrations as visual aids. Also included are instructions for making buds and leaves, as well as botanical information and folklore. Let this be a guide as you bring your own creations to life. And may your heart sing as you capture these beauties of Nature in sugar!

SPRING

ALSTROEMERIA	GARDENIA
ANEMONE	GERANIUM
BABY'S BREATH	LILY OF THE VALLEY
BELLFLOWER	MIMOSA
BLEEDING HEART	PANSY
CARNATION	ROSE
CHERRY BLOSSOM	STAR OF BETHLEHEM
DAFFODIL	SWEET PEA
DAISY	TULIP
DAPHNE	VIOLET
FORSYTHIA	

Alstroemeria in a shell vase.

Alstroemeria

ALSTROEMERIA VERSICOLOR

COMMON NAME: Peruvian Lily

A miniature lily of South America, *Alstroemeria* adds a striking accent to an arrangement due to the tigerish markings on its 3 narrow inner petals. Its threadlike stamens end with lentil-shaped tips. Flowering spring through the summer, colors include white, yellow, pink, red, and coral.

STAMENS AND PISTIL

Insert the tip of a pink mini-stamen into an extra tiny ball of moss green dough. Pinch flat. Make 6. Dust tips gray. For pistil, attach 3 pink threads to tip of a 26g wire with tape and curl slightly. Add stamens in circle.

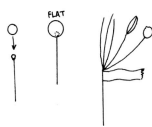

SEPALS

Roll out pink dough moderately thin and press with lily leaf veiner. Make cut with wider cutter. Thin edges with ball tool on pad and point tip with needle tool. Insert 30g wire and place upside down in curved former. Make 3 and let dry. Dust edges and base coral and points spring green.

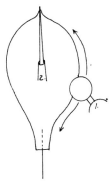

PETALS

Roll out cream dough moderately thin and cut with narrow cutter. Thin and point as before. Make 3 and let dry. Dust center lemon yellow, tip and base coral. With detail brush, paint reddish-brown stripes.

ASSEMBLY

Attach tape to wire at bottom of stamens. Join petals then sepals as in drawing.

Anemone

ANEMONE CORONARIA

COMMON NAMES: Lily of the Field, Windflower

This richly colorful wildflower from the Mediterranean springs forth in a dazzling array of blues, pinks, reds, and purples. The pink and white varieties harbor a velvety green center with golden yellow stamens. Others are black, "pupil-like" with a radius of black-tipped stamens. In Greek mythology, Anemone was a beautiful nymph who attracted the attention of Zephyr, gentle god of the West Wind. Flora, goddess of flowers, in a fit of jealous rage, transformed poor Anemone into this flower.

Anemones top a sugar display with cosmos and black-eyed Susan below.

CENTER

Form a medium ball of dark brown dough. Insert a hooked 22g wire 2½-3" (7cm) long. Slowly rotate, working bottom of ball to wire securely. Brush sides and top with glue and roll in brown to black "pollen mixture." Immediately insert 2-4 dozen purple or pink stamens, ½" (13mm) long, in a circle around sides, angled upward. Let dry. Brush stamen tips with glue and dip in same pollen mixture.

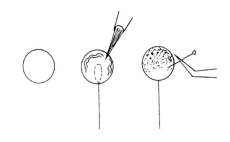

FLOWER

Cover a mug with foil, slightly cupped. Make a small hole in center. Roll out pale violet dough moderately thin. Press with petal veiner. Cut out petal and thin edges on foam pad with ball tool. Do *not* ruffle. Place in palm and cup with ball tool. Set in mug with bottom at edge of hole. Make 2 more and place in triangular fashion, attaching corners with glue at edge of hole. Make 3 more and place in between others. Lift ends slightly with fiber to cup. Brush bottom of prepared center with glue and insert wire through hole in mug. Press on top of center to secure it to petals. Let dry.

Dust base of petals dark purple, graduating outward. Lightly brush with pearl dust. (**Note:** The number of petals varies greatly with anemones, with a minimum of 6. Other varieties are found with 7, 9, or more. Use a wide cutter for the 6-petaled flower. Combine with a narrow cutter for 7 or more.)

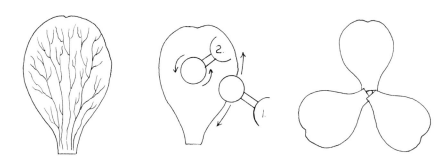

LEAVES

Roll out light green dough moderately thin. Make 3 cuts with small frilly leaf cutter. Thin and ruffle edges. Insert a 30g wire into base of each and curl downward to dry. Dust edges darker green. Attach around stem with floral tape 2-3" (5-7cm) below head of flower.

Baby's Breath

GYPSOPHILA PANICULATA

This late spring to early summer bloomer produces numerous delicate and feathery white or pink flowers. A member of the pink family, its frilly petals are formed with the same method as its cousin, the carnation. This tiny creation is a delightful contrast to any large flower.

BLOSSOMS AND BUDS

Roll out dough thin and cut with any tiny scalloped cutter. With exacto knife, cut each petal in half. On firm surface dusted with cornstarch, roll rounded toothpick back and forth around edge to frill. Brush center with glue and insert hooked 30g wire. Pinch dough together around hook. Make 3-5 blossoms of different sizes per sprig. Dust base apple green.

For buds, use tiny white stamens *or* attach an extra tiny ball of dough to tip of wire.

To form sprig, attach buds and blossoms alternately to thinnest wire. Dust wire spring green.

Bellflower

CAMPANULA

The appeal of this long-stemmed spring and summer bloomer is certainly its dangling bell-shaped flowers. The many varieties of *Campanula* ring out in pastels and vibrant shades of blue, pink, lilac, purple, and mauve as well as pure white, making it an appropriate and charming choice for wedding cakes.

CENTER

Roll an extra-small ball of yellow-green dough into a bead. Insert a hooked 26g wire into one end. With rounded scissors, make 5 snips around bead. Bend tips of snips outward. Let dry. Dust base green.

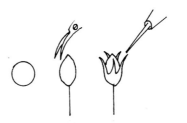

OPEN FLOWER

Prepare a large Mexican Hat with pale blue dough. Place 5-pointed cutter over hat and cut. Thin edges with ball tool on pad. Hollow out center with large ball tool to form "bell." Brush glue on prepared center and insert wire through flower to join. For calyx, roll out green dough thin. Cut with small 5-pointed cutter. Thin with ball tool and point each leg with needle tool. Insert flower wire through center and attach with glue. Let dry. Dust edges inward light blue followed by lavender. Make at least 2 per stem.

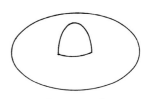

BUD

Roll a large ball of same dough into a long teardrop. Insert a hooked 26g wire into narrow end. With needle tool, make crease around bead and lines on tip as shown. For calyx, make 5 snips around base with cuticle scissors. Let dry. Dust green at base and blue down from tip. Make 1 or more per stem.

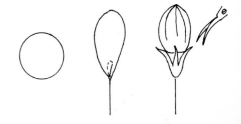

ASSEMBLY

With green floral tape, attach smallest bud to tip of a 22g wire. Continue down adding all buds followed by open flowers.

"GOLDEN YEARS"
Bleeding hearts, gardenias, sweet peas, stephanotis, and daphne ring around this sunny anniversary cake.

Bleeding Heart

DICENTRA SPECTABILIS

COMMON NAMES: Lyre Flower, Lady's Locket, and Lady in the Bath

The pendulous flowers of this late-spring arrival dangle from a woody stem in increasing sizes. The white, pink, or red heart-shaped calyx has a tiny white flower protruding from its base. What could be sweeter?

FLOWER (COROLLA)

Roll an extra-small ball of dough into a dog bone shape and point one end. Insert a 30g wire into other end. With tweezers or fingertips, pinch out flaps on sides of point. Let dry. Make 1 per flower. Dust point pink. For buds, use same shape and dust pink, leaving flaps white.

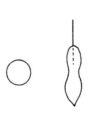

CALYX

Roll a large ball of pink dough into paddle shape. Flatten slightly on hard surface and cut handle in half. Spread snips apart and curl up. With needle tool, indent top and crease line down center. Roll ball tool around heart, mounding center. Shorten flower wire to ¼" (7mm) and insert into bottom, flaps forward and back. Insert hooked 26g wire into top indentation.

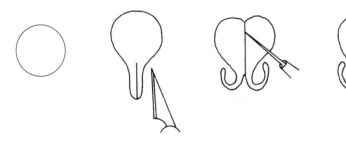

ASSEMBLY

Make as many flowers and buds as desired. For stem, attach tape to tip of a long 24g wire and join smallest bud. Add buds and flowers increasing in size. Each should dangle from a ½" (13mm) stem. Dust all stems reddish-brown.

Carnation

DIANTHUS

COMMON NAMES: Pink, Gillyflower

Since the Renaissance, this frilly flower has symbolized the happy and carefree days of spring. Its root word *carne*, meaning flesh, was chosen because the original variety was found only in pink. After centuries of cultivation, carnations now appear in red, rose, salmon, yellow, white, and bicolors. Its surprising how easily the busy ruffles are achieved simply by using a toothpick.

WIRE

Hook a 22g wire. For stamens, insert a 2" (5cm) length of cotton thread through hook. Close tightly with pliers. Wrap tape several times around wire.

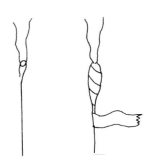

FLOWER

Roll out pink dough thin and cut out scalloped circle. Use exacto knife to cut around edge as shown. Place on hard surface dusted with cornstarch. With index finger, roll toothpick back and forth around scallops to frill. Turn over and brush center with glue up to frills. Insert wire through center and fold in half. Keep wire hidden with thread above frills. Brush glue below frills on right side and fold past center. Turn around and repeat. Pinch base to round shape.

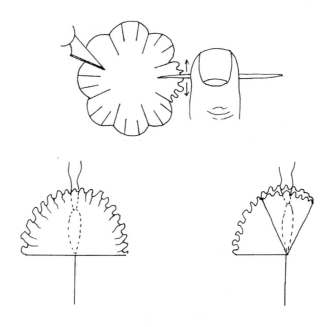

Make second cut and frill as before. Turn over, brush with glue, and slip wire through center. With index fingers and thumbs, pinch and gather second ruffle around first. Repeat for third row. Let dry. To color, hold upside down. With flat brush, dust edges darker pink. For larger flower, increase size of cutter and/or add more rows of ruffles.

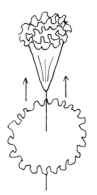

CALYX

With yellow-green dough, form a small Bowler Hat and cut out calyx. Place on pad and thin edges with ball tool. Use cone tool to hollow center. Brush inside with glue and insert flower wire to attach. With needle tool, mark lines vertically in between legs of calyx. Use cuticle scissors to cut 5 triangular indentations around base. Let dry. Dust base and edges green.

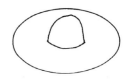

BUD

Roll a medium ball of pink dough into a stubby teardrop. Insert a hooked 22g wire into wide end. Let dry. Dust tip darker pink. Prepare smaller calyx as above. Brush inside and legs of calyx with glue and slip up wire, closing over base.

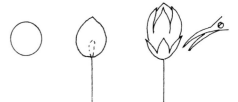

VARIATION

For mottled effect, like the Fiesta Carnation, add bits of red and yellow dough to white before rolling out.

Moments in the life of
a cherry tree are captured
on this surrealistic branch,
bearing both flowers and
fruit.

"A Binding Love"

A mutual love of classic literature inspired this romantic wedding cake, marking a new chapter in the lives
of the bride and groom. English roses, pansies, and violets are illustrated in two forms: flat-painted floodwork
and sculpted sugar dough. The arrival of a "Camberwell Beauty" butterfly adds poetry in motion.

Cherry Blossom

"The cherry blossoms open wide
In pink and white
To show their beauty."
Haiku, SCOTT WOOLLEY, age 9

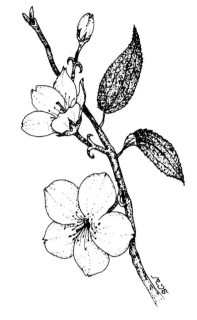

PRUNUS CERASUS

Every spring, the blossoming cherry tree is a breathtaking sight to behold. Soon countless tiny pink and white petals shower the earth, laying a magical carpet. In sugar, a branch of these blossoms is an exquisite background to any primary flowers.

CALYX

Make a small Witch's Hat with green dough and cut with tiny calyx cutter. With small ball tool, hollow out center slightly. Insert hooked 26g wire through center.

PETALS AND STAMENS

Roll out dough thin and cut with small petal cutter. With point of cutter, nick rounded edge. Cup and softly ruffle with ball tool on pad. Brush glue on back of point and attach to calyx. Make 4 more and attach.

Insert 12 white tipless stamens, ½" (13mm) long, in center. Dip ends into pink petal dust. Dust back of petals pale pink.

BUD

Roll a small ball of dough into a teardrop and insert a hooked 28g wire into point. Mark 5 lines with needle tool. Dust base spring green and tip pink. Attach blossom and bud to a 24g wire with green tape. Dust pink for woody appearance.

"She Loves Me!"
A basket cake reaching with daisies, daffodils, white forsythia, and ivy sits upon a marbleized pedestal.

Daffodil

NARCISSUS

COMMON NAME: Daffydowndilly

The advent of spring is trumpeted by the emergence of the cheery daffodil. Its botanical name comes from the Greek myth of Narcissus and Echo. Preoccupied with his own handsome form, the youth ignored the loving attention of Echo until she faded away into nothing but a distant voice. To teach him a lesson, the gods transformed him into this flower beside a lake to gaze forever at his own reflection. The legend suggests that denial of our feminine side, the yin, results in losing touch with our subconscious feelings.

PISTIL AND STAMENS

Roll an extra-small ball of yellow dough into a thin tube 1" (25mm) long. Indent one end with umbrella tool. Insert a hooked 30g wire into other end. Let dry 15 minutes. Roll a tiny ball of same dough into a long pointed teardrop. Cut almost in half as shown. Brush bottom with glue and attach to base of pistil. Repeat twice for 6 stamens. Let dry. Dust up from base apple green.

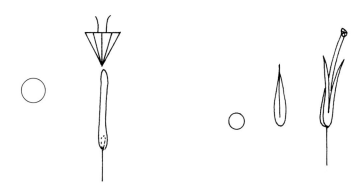

TRUMPET

Roll out same dough moderately thick and cut with trumpet cutter. Distress rounded edge with friller tool. Place on pad at edge of table and roll thin dowel back and forth to ruffle. Wrap around ½" (13mm) dowel and join sides with glue. Remove and pinch bottom to close. Insert ball tool into trumpet to round bottom. Brush glue under prepared center and insert into trumpet. Hang to dry for 1 hour. Snip off wire.

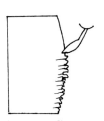

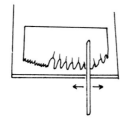

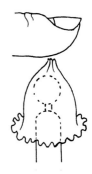

BUILDING FLOWER

Prepare a small Mexican Hat with same dough and cut with 3-petaled cutter. Press petals with corn husk and thin edges with ball tool on pad. Pinch tips to point. With ball tool, hollow out middle slightly. Insert hooked 20g wire through center. Let dry a few minutes.

Roll out same dough thin and cut with same cutter. Texture as before. Brush center of back with glue and attach to dry petals, forming 6-pointed star. Brush glue on bottom of trumpet and push into center. Let dry. Dust cone at back of flower dark green.

HOOD AND STEM

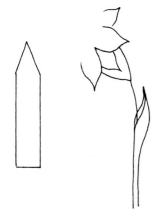

Wrap wire with white or tan tape to thicken stem. Cut a 2" (5cm) piece of tape as shown to form "hood." Wrap square end around wire and curve point over back of flower. Thicken remaining stem by attaching 2 wires with tape. Dust hood tan and bend flower downward.

LEAF

Roll a large ball of green dough into a pointed tube. Roll flat with pin with thicker bottom. Press with corn husk and enhance center vein with needle tool. Let dry. Dust dark green and tip orange.

"... she loves me,
she loves me not,
she loves me!"

Daisy

CHRYSANTHEMUM

COMMON NAMES: Thunder Flower, Ox-Eye Daisy, St. John's Flower

The name for this radiant spring flower evolved from its old English nickname "day's eye." The bright and sunny daisy evokes the spirit of innocence, making it a delightful choice for decorating cakes for children of any age.

CENTER

Flatten a medium ball of yellow dough and place on fingertip. Stretch tulle and press against dough to texture. Fold sides under to form teardrop. Insert a hooked 22g green wire into point. Tease edges outward with needle tool. Let dry. Dust mound spring green, leaving edges yellow.

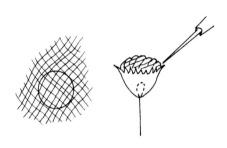

PETALS

Roll out dough moderately thick. Cut with 8-petaled cutter. With ball tool, lengthen and thin each petal on pad. Do *not* ruffle. Mark 2 or 3 lines down each petal, wiggling needle tool. Cover to prevent drying. Repeat process for second row of petals. Brush glue in center of first row and lay second on top. Press middle to join. Brush glue under prepared center. Lay petals over fingers and insert wire through middle. Turn upside down and firmly press back to secure. Insert wire into inverted trumpet flower former. Turn right side up with petals opening out. Let dry.

For calyx, dust golden brown scallops at base of petals on back and dark green near wire.

Variation: For partially open daisy, do not use former and hang upside down to dry.

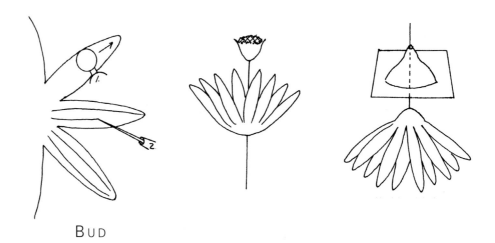

BUD

Roll a medium ball of dough into a teardrop. Insert a hooked 24g green wire into point. Indent center with umbrella tool. With needle tool, mark 6-8 lines over edge. Let dry. Dust golden brown scallop under edge and dark green at base. For leaves, use any large shaggy leaf cutter with medium green dough. Dust dark green and edge golden brown.

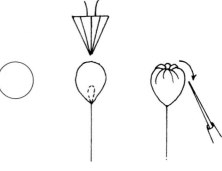

Close-up of daisies and daffodils.

Aster

Prepare daisy center and insert 12 short yellow stamens around edge. Paint stems brown. For petals, use daisy cutter only once and cut petals in half with exacto blade. Proceed as before. Colors vary from deep reds and purples to pale pinks and blues.

Black-Eyed Susan

COMMON NAME: Coneflower

State Flower of Maryland

For center, roll a medium ball of brown dough into a rounded cone. Insert a hooked 24g wire into wide end. Indent other end with umbrella tool. Brush with glue and roll in dark brown pollen mixture. Let dry.

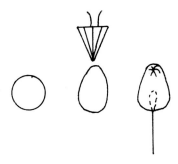

Prepare 2 rows of petals like the daisy using lemon yellow dough. Dust golden yellow.

Daphne beside an amethyst.

Daphne

DAPHNE MEZEREUM

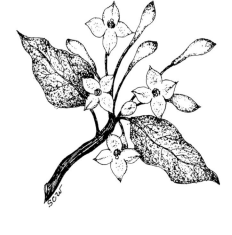

This low-lying laurel tree produces fragrant blossoms early in the spring in whites and rosy purples. According to Greek myth, the nymph, Daphne, transformed herself into this shrub to escape the passionate chase of Apollo, the Sun God.

OPEN BLOSSOM

Form dough into a small Witch's Hat and cut with 4-petaled cutter. Turn upside down on pad and thin edges with small ball tool. Open center with narrow cone tool. Insert a hooked 30g wire. With needle tool, draw vein down center of 2 petals opposite each other. Insert 1 yellow mini-stamen. Dust base spring green and back of flower pink. Make 3-5 per bunch.

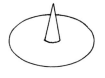

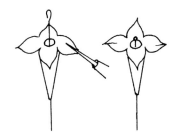

BUDS AND LEAVES

Roll small ball of dough into shape. Insert a 30g wire into narrow end. Dust base spring green and tip pink. Make 2 or 3.

Make 3-5 leaves with medium green dough. Gloss with piping gel and edge pink. To assemble, attach buds and blossoms to a 24g wire with stems of equal lengths, forming posey. Attach leaves. Dust stem reddish-brown.

Forsythia

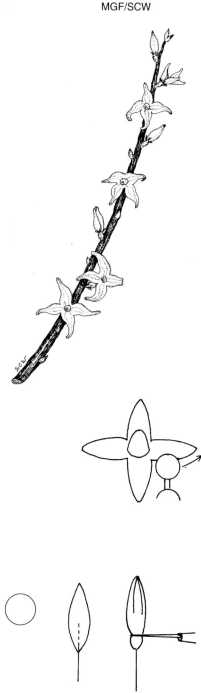

Treasured as the first shrub to bloom in early spring, this branchy bush explodes into long reaching arms of golden yellow flowerets. Originally from Asia, it was dubbed "forsythia" in honor of British botanist, William Forsyth, who encouraged cultivation in Europe. Usually yellow, there also exists a variety in white.

FLOWERS

For center stamen, dust the end of a 28g wire lemon yellow. Dampen tip with glue and dip into golden yellow pollen mixture. Make 1 per flower.

Form a tiny Mexican Hat with lemon yellow dough. Make cut with narrow 4-petaled cutter. Dip cone tool into cornstarch and then into center of hat to hollow. Thin edges with ball tool on pad and gently pinch each petal. Brush glue on stamen wire ½" (13mm) from tip and insert through hollow. Work dough to wire. Let dry. Dust hole golden yellow. With detail brush, paint a 4-pointed calyx with spring green food color on back. Make at least 3 per branch

 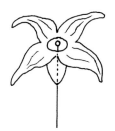 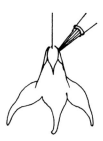

BUDS

Roll a small ball of same dough into a long bead. Insert a damp 30g wire into one end. Mark lines with needle tool, as shown. Dust and paint as above. Make at least 3 in graduating sizes per branch.

BRANCH BUDS

Roll a tiny ball of light brown dough into a teardrop. Insert a damp 30g wire into wide end. Let dry. Dust brown. Make at least 1-3 per branch.

BRANCH

With green floral tape, attach a branch bud to the tip of a 24g wire. Travel down wire, attaching flower buds increasing in size, ending with open flowers. Intersperse branch buds. Dust tape reddish-brown.

Gardenia

GARDENIA JASMINOIDES

COMMON NAME: Cape Jasmine

Known for an unforgettable sweet fragrance, this native of Africa and Asia was named in honor of botanist, Alexander Garden. Its soft creamy white petals strikingly contrast the dark glossy leaves. Flowers generally range in size from 2-3½" (5-9cm) wide. An evergreen shrub, it blooms profusely during spring and summer.

CENTER

Roll a medium ball of light cream dough into a wide softly pointed teardrop. Insert a hooked 22g wire into bottom. Indent point with umbrella tool and with needle tool, mark curved lines down sides. Dust base and center creamy yellow.

    Roll out same dough thin and make 3 cuts with smallest of 3 gardenia or dog rose cutters. With ball tool, thin center using circular motion; lightly scoot around edge for soft movement. Brush glue on lower right corner and attach to teardrop, leaving other side free. Brush glue on second petal and tuck under first, followed by third. Dust back of petals creamy yellow at base.

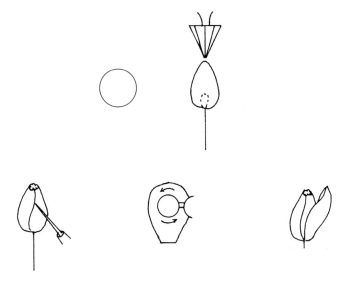

"Sweet Fragrance"
Fluffy gardenias, stephanotis, and ribbons are joined by lily of the valley piped in royal icing.

CALYX AND PETALS

Cover mug with foil and make tiny hole in center. Roll out green dough thin and cut with narrow calyx cutter. Place in center of mug.

Roll out light cream dough thin. Cut with largest cutter. Thin and softly ruffle petal as before. Turn over and tuck sides under to form a more rectangularly shaped petal. Brush glue on back at base and attach at edge of hole. Make 5 more and place around hole. Dust bottoms creamy yellow.

Hint: Uneven gaps between petals is characteristic of the gardenia.

Make 6 more petals as before using medium cutter. Attach with glue over gaps in back row. Dust as before. Brush glue under prepared center and insert through hole, pressing against petals. Let dry.

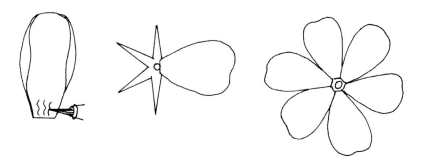

BUD

Roll a large ball of dough into a bead. Insert a hooked 24g wire into one end. Mark curved lines down sides with needle tool. Dust creamy yellow up from base and pale green down from tip. Prepare calyx as before. Insert wire through center and attach to back of bud with glue.

LEAVES

Roll out green dough moderately thin and press with strong leaf veiner. Cut 30g wire into round end. Let dry. Make at least 5 per flower. Dust dark green down center and brush with piping gel to gloss. Lightly edge burgundy. Attach in circle around flower with tape, leaving long stems.

"WINDOW DRESSER"
Geraniums flourish in royal icing soil housed in a sugar terra-cotta pot.

Geranium

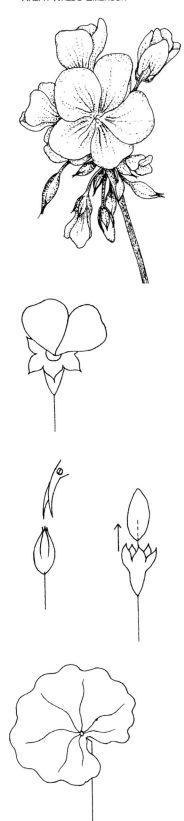

PELARGONIUM DOMESTICUM

A familiar inhabitant of window boxes worldwide, the geranium blooms atop tall slender stems with curly round leaves. An herb native to South Africa, its clusters of nodding buds unfold to form a natural bouquet of fluffy blossoms in scarlet, vermilion, salmon, and white. Symbolizing home and hospitality, this hardy plant greets us in the spring and remains a welcome guest all the way through fall.

BLOSSOMS

Form a very small Mexican Hat with green dough and cut out calyx. Thin with ball tool on pad and hollow center with cone tool. Insert hooked 26g wire. Let dry briefly.

For petals, roll out dough thin and press with delicate veiner. Cut with small teardrop cutter. Ruffle edges with ball tool. Brush glue on back of petal and attach to calyx. Make 4 more and attach, overlapping. Insert 5 short mini-stamens into center. Make 7 or more for full bouquet. Dust inward from edges pink, leaving center white.

BUDS

For closed buds, form a small teardrop with green dough and insert a 26g wire into bottom. Snip the tip with cuticle scissors twice. Dust tip pink. Make at least 3.

For opening bud, form a small bead of dough and insert wire into either end. Let dry. Dust tip pink. Form calyx as above and insert bead wire through center, attaching with glue. Make 3 or more.

For unfolding buds, wrap 1 or 2 petals around bead before attaching calyx. Make 2 or more.

LEAVES

Roll out green dough moderately thin and press with veiner. Cut with round scalloped cutter and snip out small triangle. Strongly ruffle edges with ball tool on pad. Insert 24g wire into center. Let dry. Bend wire under. Dust darker green and edge pink. Make 5 or more in 2 or 3 different sizes.

ASSEMBLY

Attach green floral tape to the tip of a long 20g wire and wrap first blossom with a 1½" (4cm) stem. Continue adding blossoms forming bouquet and end with buds at bottom. Bend buds downward. Attach leaves near base with smallest first.

"CLEOPATRA'S VALLEY"

A Cleopatra butterfly perches on the edge of a pastoral wedding cake. Top tier basket holds roses, stephanotis, freesia, baby's breath, and delicate lily of the valley.

Lily of the Valley

CONVALLARIA MAJALIS

COMMON NAMES: Jacob's Tears, Ladder to Heaven

This sweetly fragrant spring flower produces large bluish green leaves that envelop thin stalks of white bell-shaped blossoms. Stems range from 4-8" (10-20cm) in height, suspending 6-12 dangling flowers. According to folklore, this delicate beauty was believed to have the power to inspire visions of a better world.

BLOSSOMS

Form a tiny ball of dough. Hollow out slightly with tiny ball tool. For scalloped edge, press ball tool inside bell 5 times around edge. Dip tip of white mini-stamen into glue and insert. Make 6-12 per stem. For buds, use large-tipped white stamens.

LEAVES

Roll out bluish green dough moderately thick and press with corn husk. Cut with lily petal cutter. Thin edges on pad with ball tool. Insert 24g wire into bottom. Point and line center vein with needle tool. Dry with tip curving back on fiber. Dust dark green and edge pink. Make 1 or 2 per bunch.

ASSEMBLY

Attach tape to end of 26g wire and join bud. Continue down, attaching buds, then flowers left and right. Dust wires spring green. Attach bottom of stems to leaf wires with tape.

"TENDER FEELINGS"
Sprigs of mimosa dot clusters of wild roses, sweet peas, violets, and long spiraling tendrils of ivy.

Mimosa

"Spring hangs her infant blossoms on the trees, Rock'd in the cradle of the western breeze."
WILLIAM COWPER

ACACIA

COMMON NAME: Wattle

Australia is the origin of this delicate evergreen tree, which produces abundant flower clusters of white, pink, and lemon yellow, the most common variety. Because of their shape, these flowers add a lovely pearl-like quality to a bridal bouquet or wedding arrangement. Mimosa has also been used internationally as a symbol of the women's movement to honor the feminine energies.

FLOWERS AND BUDS

Form at least 7 medium, small, or extra-small balls of lemon yellow dough. Insert a damp 30g wire 1½" (4cm) long into each. Let dry. Brush with glue and roll in lemon yellow pollen mixture.

Form at least 5 tiny and extra-tiny balls of apple green dough. Insert wire as above and let dry. Brush with glue and roll *half* in lemon yellow pollen mixture and *half* in apple green. This creates 3 stages of the mimosa.

LEAVES

Roll out light green dough moderately thin and press with corn husk or veiner. With circular blade, cut out narrow pointed leaves 1½-2" (4-5cm) long. Thin edge with ball tool on pad and insert damp 30g wire. Draw line down center with needle tool. Let dry flat. Dust powdery blue-green and edge with golden brown. Make 3 or more.

ASSEMBLY

Attach the smallest green ball to the tip of a 28g wire with floral tape. Travel down wire, attaching balls in increasing sizes, forming a cluster near base. Attach leaves to main stem in a left and right fashion. Dust stem reddish-brown.

Pansy

VIOLA TRICOLOR HORTENSIS

COMMON NAMES: Peeping Tom, Monkey Faces, Three Face in a Hood

Deriving its name from the French word *pensée*, meaning thought, this hardy garden flower has come to symbolize "thinking of you." According to legend, it was originally white until pierced by Cupid's arrow, inspiring Oberon's line from *A Midsummer Night's Dream*. The pansy was believed to have the power to ease the hearts of separated lovers, coining another name, Heartsease. A tricolored pansy is described here.

"PANSY GARDEN"
Pickets and pebbles of sugar dough edge a cake of pansies, fiddlehead and arrowhead ferns. Stray buttercups and a snail enliven the setting laden with sugary stones and royal icing mortar.

CALYX

Form a small Mexican Hat with green dough and cut out calyx. Thin with ball tool on pad and hollow out center lightly. Insert hooked 26g wire through center. Let dry. Dust back dark green and edges pink.

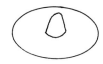

  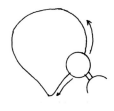

TOP PETALS

Roll out violet dough thin and press with fine veiner. Cut with large teardrop cutter. Thin edges with ball tool on pad. Attach to upper left of calyx with glue. Repeat for second petal and attach overlapping first.

SIDE AND BOTTOM PETALS

Roll out white dough thin and make cut with small teardrop cutter. Attach with glue as shown. Repeat for second petal and attach opposite first.

Roll out yellow dough thin and press with veiner. Cut with heart cutter and attach to bottom of calyx.

For center, roll an extra tiny ball of dough into a "U" shape. Attach upside down above middle with glue.

With detail brush, paint violet lines on 3 bottom petals as shown. Dust top 2 petals purple and golden yellow under "U."

  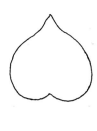 

LEAVES

Roll out medium green dough moderately thin and cut with narrow leaf cutter with jagged edges. Enhance center vein with needle tool and fold in half. Dust dark green and gloss. Edge red.

"CASCADE OF ROSES"
A pattern piped in royal icing echoes the rose motif. Sweet peas, ivy, and tiny buds of pearlbush spill down the tiers.

Rose

ROSA

Possibly the oldest of cultivated flowers, the rose has symbolized beauty and elegance throughout history. In Greek mythology, Chloris, goddess of the flowers, crowned the rose queen of all she tended. With over 200 different species, varying in form, color, and number of petals, this beloved flower offers unlimited possibilities to the sugar artist. Described here is the classic "Peace" rose with its glowing yellow center and soft pink edges.

BASE

Form a big ball of light yellow dough into teardrop. Insert a damp hooked 20g wire into wide end. Rotate slowly and work bottom to wire. With needle tool, mark hip at base. Let dry 24-48 hours. Dust base lemon yellow and tip pink.

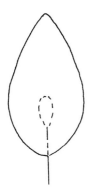
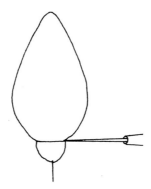

PETALS

Roll out same dough very thin. Make cut with smaller of 2 rose petal cutters. On pad, run ball tool softly over center in circular motion; thin edge but do *not* ruffle. Brush glue on lower half and wrap around prepared base, just above tip. After each row of petals, dust back yellow and edge pink.

For second row, cut 2 petals and use ball tool as before. Brush glue on lower right side and attach to base, leaving other side free. Brush glue on second petal and tuck under first. Secure open sides to base with glue.

Important: Forming each row will be easier if you press left side of petal very firmly against base when attaching, especially for last rows.

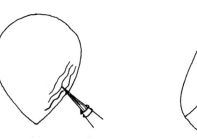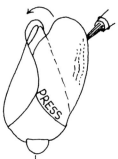

For third row, cut 3 petals. Work and attach as before.

For fourth row, lighten dough by adding white. Cut 4 petals with larger cutter. With ball tool, softly ruffle edges by using more pressure. Attach as before *except* flip petal before brushing with glue. Forming the last 2 rows in this way will create the look of an opening rose.

For fifth row, lighten dough again and cut 5 large petals. Attach as 4th row, holding rose upside down.

Close up of roses.

Calyx

Roll out light green dough moderately thin. Make cut with 5-pointed cutter. With exacto knife, cut short diagonal slits, as in diagram. With ball tool, thin edges and point tips with needle tool. Flip and brush glue in center and at base of each leg. Insert flower wire through center of calyx and attach over hip. Curl points downward. With needle tool, enhance line around hip. Let dry. Dust base dark green and edge pink.

 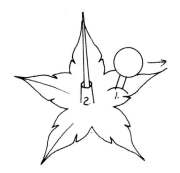 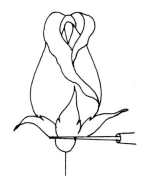

Bud

Form a large ball of yellow dough into shape, as in diagram, inserting 22g wire. Form and attach calyx as before, closing points around bud. Dust as before.

  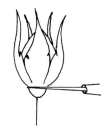

Leaves

Roll out green dough moderately thin and press with veiner. Make cut with rose leaf cutter. Thin edge on pad with ball tool, no ruffles. Insert a damp 30g green wire into base. Let dry. Dust darker green and brush with piping gel loosened with water. Let dry. Edge deep red.

Variations

For smaller rose, omit 4th row. Always end a row with an odd number of petals. For a tight, wrapped look, use only 1 large and wide rose petal cutter and omit 4th and 5th rows. Instead, flip petals of 3rd row.

For a red, red rose, use a deep red dough. Dust with red and then lightly brush and edge with violet.

"PATIO PLANTER"
Star of Bethlehem, daffodils, and Johnny-jump-ups appear to grow from a basket cake sitting on a board
decorated with flowed sugar bricks.

*"O holy night!
The stars are brightly shining!"*
Traditional Carol

Star of Bethlehem

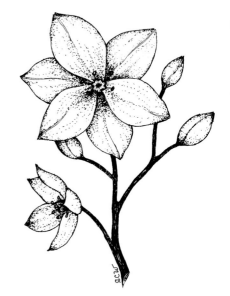

ORNITHOGALUM UMBELLATUM

The appearance of this "Star" after the last snow has melted assures us that spring is undeniably here. A member of the lily family, the flower opens late in the morning and closes at dusk. Clusters of these pure white blossoms complement any bridal bouquet.

CENTER

Roll a small ball of pale green dough into a stubby bead. Insert a hooked 26g wire and indent with umbrella tool. With tweezers, pinch 5 ridges. Insert short yellow mini-stamen at base of each ridge. Let dry.

PETALS

Roll out dough thin and cut with triple petal cutter. On pad, point tips with needle tool, enhancing center vein. Place in small trumpet former. Make second cut and brush with glue to attach to first. Brush glue under prepared center and insert wire through former. Let dry. Dust back of first petals green.

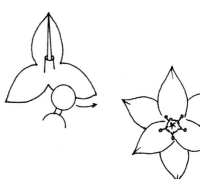

BUD

Roll a medium ball of dough into a wide bead. Insert hooked 26g wire. With needle tool, draw 3 lines from tip to base. Dust up from base spring green, leaving tip white.

95

"SWEET P'S"

Sweet peas make a cameo appearance on an oval cake covered with marbleized fondant and decorated with floodwork letters and gum paste pearls.

Sweet Pea

LATHYRUS ODORATUS

A cousin of the edible pea, this delightfully fragrant climber produces tissuey petals in every color except yellow. In a bunch or grouped with other flowers, their busy ruffles always add movement and charm.

BASE OR BUD

Roll a medium ball of dough into a long teardrop. Flatten slightly on pad and ruffle one side with ball tool. Insert a hooked 26g wire. Let dry. Dust apple green at base, tip and edges pink and violet. For bud, add calyx.

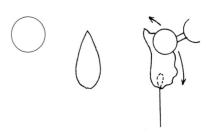

PETALS

Roll out dough thin and press with fine veiner. Cut with "wing" cutter. Ruffle edges with ball tool. Brush center with glue and attach to back of bud. Let dry forward.

   Roll out dough thin and vein. Cut with wide cutter and ruffle as before. Fold in half to crease. Open and brush glue below center and attach to back of flower. Bend top and sides back. Let dry and dust as bud.

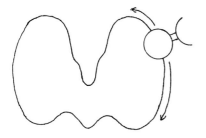
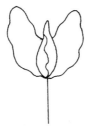
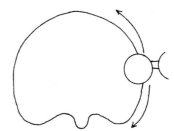

CALYX

Roll out green dough thin and cut out calyx. Point each leg with needle tool. Insert flower wire and attach to base with glue. Dust edges pink.

STEM

Attach tendril (see IVY) to the tip of a long 24g wire with green tape. Join bud with short stem. Move down 1" (25mm) and join open flower.

SIDE VIEW

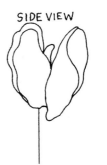

Tulip

TULIPA

Originally cultivated in Turkey, this flower derived its name from the Turkish word *tulibend* meaning turban, which it was said to resemble. For generations, tulips have symbolized perfect love and have even been used in love potions. Described here are 6 different versions of Holland's beloved flower in all of its stages.

Turkish, Parrot, and Rembrandt tulips burst open in a ceramic vase—a floral arrangement that will last for years.

BUD OR BASE

Roll a big ball of dough into a teardrop. Insert a hooked 20g wire into bottom. Slowly rotate and work to wire. With needle tool, mark 3 deep creases from tip to base, as shown. Lay on side. With friller tool, open tip mashing dough outward. Let dry. For bud, use green dough. Dust base darker green and tip any color. For closed tulip, use desired color dough. Dust darker shade at base and tip. Petals will be added as below.

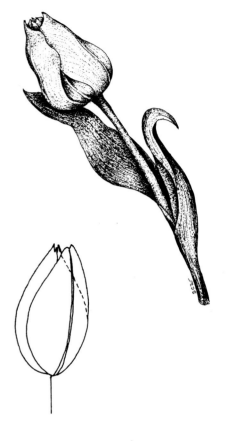

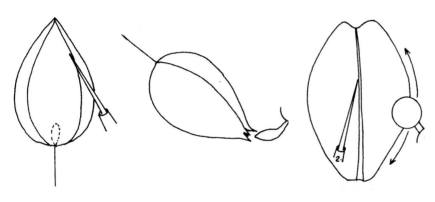

CLOSED TULIP

Roll out dough thin and cut out petal. Press with veiner or draw 2 parallel lines down center with needle tool. Thin edges on pad with ball tool. Brush glue at base and halfway up center. Attach over creased line on prepared base, bending tip out. Make 2 more petals and attach as before, overlapping as in drawing. Let dry. Dust base and edges darker shade. Pearlize.

Open Parrot Tulip

CENTER

For pistil, roll a medium ball of light green dough into "light bulb" shape. Insert a hooked 24g wire into narrow end. With tweezers, pinch 3 wide ridges around top. Pinch both sides of each to form double flaps. Let dry. Dust base dark green. Brush flaps with glue and dip into yellow pollen mixture.

For stamens, roll a tiny ball of same dough into a long bead. Insert a 30g wire into one end. Make 6. Let dry. Brush with glue and dip into orange pollen mixture. Wrap tape around wire below pistil and attach stamens in a circle.

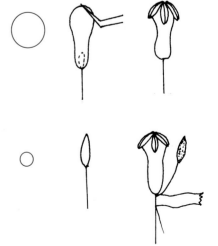

PETALS

Roll out pale pink dough moderately thin and cut petal. Texture as with closed tulip, then mash outside edge with friller tool. Ruffle frilled edge with dowel, rolling back and forth on pad near edge of table. Insert a 28g wire into base. To dry, place in egg carton or on fiber to cup. Make 6. Dust base apple green and edges deeper pink. Pearlize. To assemble, bend 3 petals back and attach to pistil wire with tape. Repeat with other 3 petals, placed in between inner row.

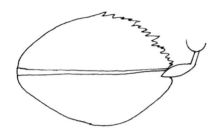 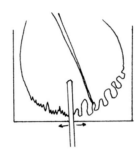 

Open Common Tulip: Use same method as Parrot but do *not* frill or ruffle edges.

Rembrandt Tulip: Prepare Common Tulip and paint feathery pattern with red food color as shown.

Turkish or Lily-Flowered Tulip: For closed flower, prepare elongated base and attach 3 petals using tiger lily cutter. Curve back and point petal tips. For open tulip, make 6 petals using 28g wire.

 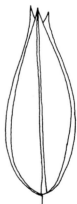

REMBRANDT   TURKISH

LEAVES

Roll out thick strip of bluish-green dough. Texture with corn husk or veiner. With circular blade, cut out a wide feather shape 4-6" (10-15cm) long. With ball tool, thin edges on pad. Insert a 22g wire into base. With needle tool, draw center vein. Shape and let dry on fiber. Dust apple green followed by white to create dusty look. Edge pink.

Violet

VIOLA ODORATA

State Flower of Illinois, New Jersey, Rhode Island, and Wisconsin

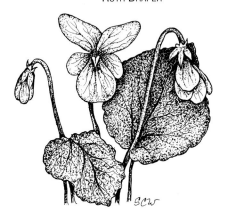
The adorable little flower whose color is the same as its name may also be found in varieties that are white, pink, yellow, and blue. Magically turn a simple ball of dough into a heartrending effect without a cutter. The pulled flower method is used to form this sweet, sweet violet.

METHOD

Roll a large ball of pale violet dough into a long teardrop. Insert a cone tool into wide end. With exacto knife, make 2 cuts for large bottom petal a quarter of the way around edge. Divide remainder with 3 evenly spaced cuts. Remove tool and open petals outward. Gently pinch corners to round. Pinch and pull petals outward, lengthening 2 upper petals. On pad, thin edges with ball tool. Pinch back to narrow flower. Curve a hooked 28g wire and insert through center and out behind top petals. Bend back of flower downward.

BEAK AND CALYX

Roll a tiny ball of golden yellow dough into a pointed teardrop. Brush glue at center of petals and attach "beak."

Roll out green dough thin and cut out tiny calyx. Attach to back of flower with glue.

FINISHING TOUCH

With detail brush, paint violet lines as shown. Dust petals pink, then dark violet.

LEAVES

Roll out green dough moderately thin and press with strong leaf veiner. Cut with heart cutter. Ruffle edges on pad with ball tool. Insert 30g wire opposite point. Shape in trumpet former. Let dry. Dust center dark green. Brush with piping gel to gloss. Dust edge pink or red.

Voila! A Viola!

Sweet violets (previous page), lilies, and ivy gather together in Blythe's birthday basket, dripping with piped lilacs and lily of the valley.

"MIRACLE OF THE LOTUS" Buttercups, jasmine and lotus flowers sip from this placid Japanese water garden.

SUMMER

BUTTERCUP	HIBISCUS	STEPHANOTIS
CALLA LILY	IRIS	SUNFLOWER
CLEMATIS	MORNING GLORY	TUBEROSE
DAYLILY	ORIENTAL LILY	WATER LILY
GALLICA ROSE	POPPY	WILD ROSE

"The buttercup catches the sun in its chalice."
JAMES LOWELL

Buttercup

RANUNCULUS ACRIS

COMMON NAMES: Gold Cup, King Cup

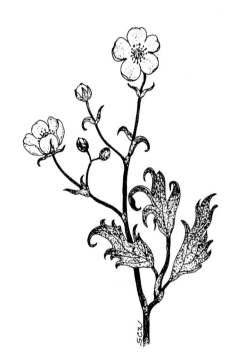

As children, we hold this sunny little flower under someone's chin to see the reflection of its golden glow. Clusters of buttercups dot low-lying grasses of lawns and meadows in the early days of summer. As a sugar decoration for children's cakes, it's cute as a bug's ear.

FORMING FLOWERS

For stamen center, attach an extra-tiny ball of light green dough onto the tip of a 28g green wire. Let dry. Brush with glue and dip into apple green pollen mixture.

Roll out yellow dough moderately thin. Use a rounded 5-petal cutter, ½" (13mm) diameter. Then cut out a tiny triangle at edge of each petal with any pointed cutter. Thin edges with medium ball tool. Cup each petal in palm with small ball tool. Brush glue under prepared center and insert wire through petals. Let dry. Brush petals with piping gel loosened with water for shiny appearance.

For leaf, use any tiny shaggy leaf cutter with spring green dough.

Sugar calla lilies are always in bloom!

Calla Lily

ZANTEDESCHIA AETHIOPICA

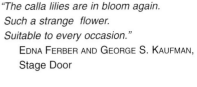

"The calla lilies are in bloom again.
Such a strange flower.
Suitable to every occasion."
    EDNA FERBER AND GEORGE S. KAUFMAN,
    Stage Door

COMMON NAMES: Arum Lily, Lily of the Nile

This white trumpet flower that proclaims joy whenever displayed is always an elegant choice. Its gracefully wrapped spathe, the outer bract or leaf, surrounds a yellow tubular spadix. Other varieties of this early summer bloomer are wrapped in pink, red, yellow, apricot, and lavender.

SPADIX

Roll a medium ball of golden yellow dough into a tube 2" (5cm) long with one wider end. Insert hooked 22g wire. Let dry. Except for base, brush with glue and roll in granulated sugar.

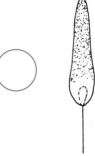

BRACT

Roll out dough moderately thin and press with arum or orchid veiner. Cut with calla lily cutter. On pad, thin edge with ball tool and point with needle tool. Brush glue at bottom and ¾" (2cm) up on left side and wrap around bottom of spadix. Brush glue up right side and fold over left. Place in trumpet former or curve on fiber. Dust inside hollow lemon yellow. Outside, dust apple green up from base and dark green near wire. (For large lily, make template with enlarged cutter shape. Hang upside down to dry.)

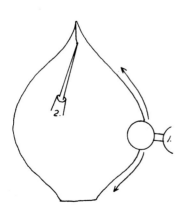

Now that's what I call a lily!

"Nature Lovers"
Clematis, bleeding heart, and viola climb over softly rounded tiers bordered with royal icing flounces.

Clematis

Often called "Queen of the Climbers," this garden vine blooms profusely in the summer shade in every imaginable color. The number of sepals differs among the many varieties, some having as few as 4. The following process forms a 7-sepaled blossom with a blush of pink, encircling a spidery yellow center. What a romantic choice for an outdoor wedding!

CENTER

Roll a medium ball of cream dough into a teardrop. Insert a hooked 26g wire into point. Indent with umbrella tool. Let dry. Roll out dough thin and cut with small daisy cutter. With needle tool, point and curl by drawing line down center. Insert wire through center and attach with glue, curling legs up. Repeat. With larger cutter, add 2 rows, forming small spider mum. Let dry. Dust tips golden yellow.

SEPALS

Roll out white dough thin and cut with clematis or lily cutter. Thin edges on pad with ball tool. Insert a 28g wire. Draw 3 lines down center with needle tool. Pinch tip to point. Let dry flat. Make 7. Dust base apple green, edges and tips soft pink.

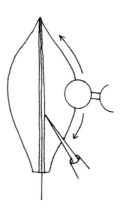

ASSEMBLY

Wrap green tape to wire under center. Bend each sepal wire to a right angle and attach in circle.

"To Hearts Combined"
Daylilies and pansies harmonize in a wedding basket trailing with vines of heart-shaped ivy.

Daylily

HEMEROCALLIS

This lily of America's woods, whose blooms last for only a single day, has been crossbred to achieve a multitude of vivid colors. Its wide ruffled petals surround slender curved pistil and stamens. The method below forms a lily quickly without individually wired petals.

PISTIL AND STAMENS

Roll a tiny ball of green dough into a teardrop and insert 30g wire into point. Make 3 pinches around top with tweezers. Dust 6 25g wires green at base to yellow at top. Dip tips into glue and into orange pollen mixture. Attach tape to pistil and join in circle and curve. Attach ring of green dough 2" (5cm) below tips with glue.

PETALS

Roll out pale yellow dough thin and press with lily petal veiner. Cut with narrow cutter. Thin edges with ball tool on pad and point tip with needle tool. Place into large trumpet former, curving petal back. Repeat for 2 more, forming triangle. Cut out 3 petals with wide cutter. Ruffle edges with small ball tool. Brush glue on back of base and attach in between petals in former. Brush glue under ring and insert through petals, pulling ring into flower. Let dry. Dust hollow light green and rest of petals yellow.

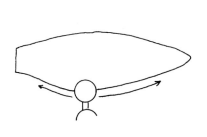
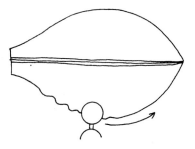

"*PASSIONATE LOVE*"

Five tiers stacked high form an exciting edifice of cake. Here, a floral pattern matching the bridal gown sets off fiery fiesta carnations and giant gallica roses.

Gallica Rose

The oldest of all garden roses, the gallica blooms in June and is known for its large open flowers and long-lasting fragrance. Brought to England and France by the Crusaders, one variety, "the Red Rose of Lancaster," has ruffled petals surrounding a golden center with yellow stamens tipped in red.

CENTER

Roll a medium ball of yellow dough into a teardrop. Insert a hooked 22g wire into point. Indent other end with umbrella tool and distress upper edge with needle tool. Insert 12 tipless yellow stamens ⅜" (1cm) long, into center and 24 or more stamens ¾" (2cm) long with tips around edge. Let dry. Paint tips of stamens red.

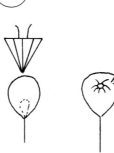

PETALS

Prepare mug with foil sunken in slightly. Make hole in center. Roll out green dough moderately thin and make cut with calyx cutter. Place in mug and make hole in center. Roll out red dough thin. With largest of 3 dog rose cutters, make 5 cuts. Thin and ruffle edges with ball tool on pad. Place overlapping petals in mug around hole and attach with glue. Prepare second row of petals as above with medium cutter and third row with smallest. Lift with fiber to individuate. Brush glue under prepared center and insert wire through hole. Press to join. Let dry. Dust petals red and edge purple.

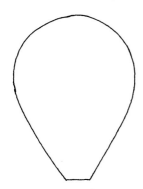
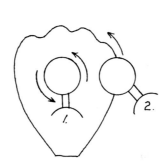

Hibiscus

ROSA SINENSIS

COMMON NAMES: Flower of an Hour, Rose of Sharon, Good Night at Noon

Originally from China, this gorgeous flower has found its home in the tropical climates of the world. A Hawaiian favorite, it is often used to chain the traditional island leis. Usually seen in stunning shades of red, yellow, orange, pink, lavender, and blue, blossoms can even be found as large as 15" (38cm) in diameter.

"PEARL ANNIVERSARY"
Wavy flounces billow beneath a sugary seascape on this cake celebrating 30 years. Flowers, oyster, pearls, and starfish were modeled in gum paste with royal icing coral, and raw sugar (turbinado) used as a sandy background.

PISTIL AND STAMENS

Roll a medium ball of dough into a tube 2" (5cm) long, wider at one end. Insert 22g wire into wide end. Insert 5 large-tipped pink stamens ½" (13mm) long into other end. With tweezers, insert 18-24 yellow mini-stamens ⅜" (1cm) long on sides near tip. Let dry straight. Dust magenta up from base. Brush tips of mini-stamens with glue and dip into yellow pollen mixture.

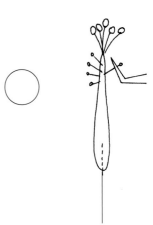

CALYX AND PETALS

For calyx, roll out green dough thin and cut with small calyx cutter. Place in bottom of large trumpet former. Poke hole in center with needle tool.

For petals, roll out pale pink dough thin. Press with delicate veiner. Cut petal with hibiscus or large dog rose cutter. Thin and ruffle outer edge with ball tool on pad. Brush glue on back of base and attach to calyx in former. Make 4 more and overlap with last petal tucked under first. Dust magenta up from base of each petal. Brush glue on bottom of pistil and insert into flower, pulling wire to secure. Let dry. Dust edges pink and base of calyx dark green. Pearlize.

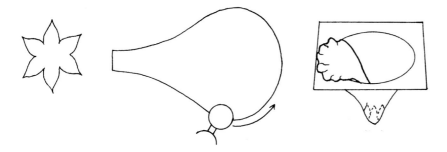

BUD

Roll a large ball of pale pink dough into a long teardrop. Insert a hooked 22g wire into wide end. Wrap 2 or 3 petals around teardrop, attaching with glue. Attach calyx at base. Let dry. Dust as before.

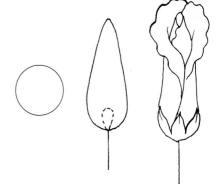

LEAVES

Roll out dark green dough thin and cut with jagged leaf cutter. Brush with piping gel for glossy texture. Edge magenta.

Oyster and Pearl

Dot a large ball of dough with black food paste color. Mix in unevenly and form into oval for bottom of shell. Pinch edges thin. Dampen and insert 2 short L-shaped wires (20g) into back edge to support top of shell. Form top as before and insert back edge into wires, propping open with fiber. Let dry several hours. Dust edges black and pearlize entire shell.

For flesh, mold light tan dough into a flat oval and place inside shell with glue. Mold a second smaller oval, ruffling edge with ball tool. Attach on top. Dust ruffle brown and glaze with piping gel for wet look.

For pearl, form small ball of dough. Let dry, then pearlize and place inside oyster.

Starfish

Form a mound of golden brown dough and cut with any 5-pointed cutter. Indent center with umbrella tool and texture surface by poking with tip #15. Let dry. Dust bottom edge darker brown, then pipe tiny dots of royal icing over entire surface.

Coral

Tape a large square of wax paper 5 x 5" (13 x 13cm) to a flat surface. With royal icing, pipe "tree" shape using tip #6 for main stem, then tip #4 and #2 for smaller and finer branches. Insert toothpick into main stem. Make 3 or more and let dry several hours. Carefully remove from wax paper and insert toothpicks into cake, placing branches   at different angles.

Sand

Simply use turbinado (raw sugar) or color granulated sugar tan. Work a teaspoon or two of egg white into sugar with hands and sprinkle on cake to prevent "sand" from shifting.

Iris

IRIS GERMANICA

COMMON NAME: Flags

Iris is also defined as a rainbowlike display of colors, which certainly applies to the many varieties of genus *Iris*. According to legend, the Greek goddess, Iris, used the rainbow as a bridge to take important messages of love from the "eye of Heaven" to the earth. The three lower petals have come to symbolize the virtues of faith, wisdom, and valor, and inspired the classic French *fleur-de-lis*.

TOP PETALS (STANDARDS)

Roll out dough moderately thin and press with delicate veiner. Cut with medium dog rose cutter. On pad, thin and strongly ruffle edge with medium ball tool. Turn over. With needle tool, draw line down center. Insert a 30g wire into base. Let dry on fiber with ruffle curving back. Make 3. Dust base apple green.

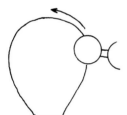  

MIDDLE PETALS

Roll out dough moderately thin and make cut with small dog rose cutter. Split petal with exacto knife as shown. On pad, thin edges with medium ball tool. To cup upper area, roll medium ball tool back and forth in palm. Insert 30g wire into base. With tweezers, pinch double ridge at base. Let dry with upper area bending back. Make 3. Dust edges violet and pink. Brush ridges with glue and sprinkle with yellow pollen mixture.

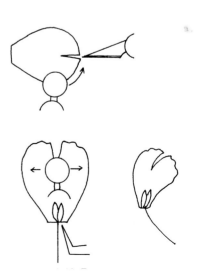

A noble iris rises from a sugar cube.

Lower Petals (Falls)

Roll out dough moderately thin. Press with veiner and cut with large dog rose cutter. Ruffle edges strongly on pad with medium ball tool. Insert a 30g wire. Enhance center veins with needle tool. Let dry on fiber, curving down. For "beard," roll a tiny ball of dough into a pointed bead. Glue to base of petal. Tease edges with needle tool for rough texture. Make 3. Dust ruffled edges violet and pink. Brush beard with glue and sprinkle with yellow pollen mixture.

Assembly

Attach tape to tip of 22g wire and wrap top petals vertically, curving in. Bend wires of middle petals to a 90° angle and attach below and in between top petals. Bend wires of lower petals as before and attach under middle petals.

Stem and Leaves

For stem, roll out a narrow strip of green dough ⅜" (1cm) wide. Brush glue on underside and wrap around wire. Cut out a triangle of beige dough. Attach to stem below petals, bending tip outward. Dust edge of triangle golden brown.

For leaves, roll out green dough moderately thin. With circular blade, cut a long pointed triangle(½" (13mm) wide. Texture with corn husk or veiner. Thin edges with ball tool and with needle tool, enhance center vein down leaf. Let dry. Dust darker green and edge golden brown.

Ode to an Iris

Oh, fabulous confection!
You lift your frilly arms
And dip your lacy petticoat—
A can-can tootsie,
A bauble—dimpled, boldly painted, too;
I look away:
Your beauty teases and causes me to blush.

Oh, regal crest!
You raise your prayerful arms
And unfold your richest robes
A pied beauty,
A royal priest, bedecked to celebrate Laetare.
I fix on you:
How can you be so much at once?

Patricia M. Connolly
(Composed after receiving the gift of a sugar iris)

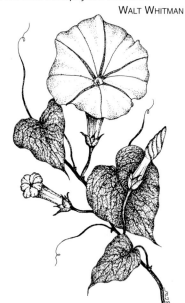

Morning Glory

IPOMOEA

Originally from Mexico, this glorious vine opens its trumpetlike blossoms each day at sunrise and closes them by midafternoon. One white variety, called "Moonflower," opens at nightfall to enjoy the moonlight as well as the morning sun. Here's how to form a moonflower in its three stages.

STAMENS

Wrap 6 white mini-stamens 1" (25mm) long to the end of a 24g wire with tape. Dust stems apple green.

"MOON FLOWERS"
A profile of Diana, goddess of the moon, is framed by a silvery cake collar of floodwork. Indigo fondant covers cake and board.

OPEN FLOWER

Form a large Witch's Hat and cut with circle cutter 1½-2" (4-5cm) diameter. On page, thin and ruffle edges with ball tool. Hollow out center with narrow cone tool. Hold between index finger and thumb and mark 5 deep lines from center to edge. Then lightly mark another line in between each of those. Brush glue below stamens and insert wire through hollow. Stamens should not protrude. Dust hollow and deep lines apple green. Pearlize.

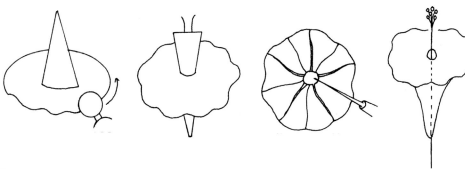

CALYX

Roll out medium green dough thin and cut with small 5-pointed cutter. Insert flower wire through center and attach with glue. Dust dark green and edge pink.

BUD

Roll a large ball of dough into a dog bone and point one end. Insert a hooked 24g wire into other end. With needle tool, mark 2 or 3 lines down point and twist. Attach calyx as above.

CLOSED FLOWER

Roll a large ball of dough into a dog bone. Indent one end with umbrella tool. Insert a hooked 24g wire into other end. With needle tool, mark 10 lines over edge. Attach calyx as before. Dust center apple green.

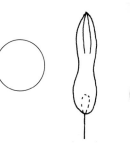

LEAVES

Make 3 different sizes of heart-shaped leaves with medium green dough. Gloss with piping gel. Form vine interspersing flowers and buds throughout. Wrap stem with green tape and dust burgundy.

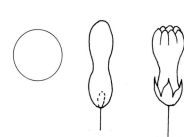

"Stargazers"

Colorful Oriental lilies contrast pastel roses and dendrobium orchids crowding the ledges of this striking wedding cake. Baby's breath, blossoms and eucalyptus leaves fill out the arrangements.

Oriental Lily

LILIUM

This group of spectacular lilies from the East blooms in late summer, producing showy flowers that exude a powerful vanilla perfume. Examples include the white "CasaBlanca" and such speckled varieties as the crimson "Stargazer" and, a favorite of brides, the pink and white "Rubrum Lily."

PISTIL

Roll a medium ball of dough into a tube 2½" (6cm) long with bulbous end. With tweezers, pinch 3 ridges. Insert 24g wire into other end. Dry curved on flat surface. Dust tip spring green, middle apple green and leave bottom white. Paint ridges dark brown.

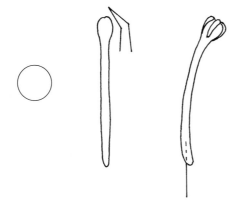

STAMENS

Roll a tiny ball of dough into a bead. Insert 30g wire into middle. Pinch underneath to join. Curve to dry. Make 6. Dust stems apple green. Brush with glue and dip tips into rust colored pollen mixture. Wrap tape to pistil wire and attach stamens in circle.

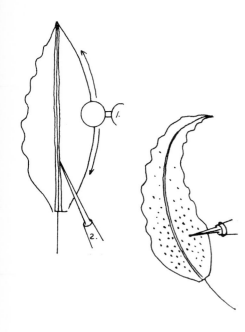

PETALS

Roll out dough moderately thin and press with lily veiner. Cut with wide cutter. With ball tool, ruffle edges on pad. Insert a 28g wire and dry on fiber, curling tip under. Make 3.

Repeat with narrow cutter, ruffling edges more. Dust a narrow triangle at base apple green and rest of petal pink. With detail brush, paint dark pink dots profusely. Keep edges white. Make 3. For "Stargazer," dust stronger pink, then red above triangle. Paint dots dark red.

Rubrum lily on plaque.

ASSEMBLY

Attach 3 wide petals around base of pistil with tape. Secure by wrapping tape down wire. Reattach at base and add 3 narrow petals under and between first.

BUD

Roll a big ball of dough into shape as shown. Insert hooked 22g wire. With needle tool, draw 3 deep lines from tip to base. Let dry. Dust apple green on lines and at base, pink in between lines.

LEAVES

Roll out green dough moderately thin and press with lily leaf veiner. Cut with pointed leaf cutter or freehand with circular blade. Thin edges with ball tool on pad. Insert 30g wire. Curve to dry. Dust center darker green and gloss with piping gel. Edge pink.

Field Lily

Wild lilies of the field are seen in every hue but blue. One orange variety, commonly known as the tiger lily, is formed like the Oriental lily with the following adjustments.

Use light orange dough to form petals. Do not ruffle edges. Dust darker orange and paint speckles dark brown. For pistil, dust orange down from tip. Use dark brown pollen mixture for stamen tips.

A stalk of foxglove stands tall behind a tiger lily and scarlet poppy.

Poppy

PAPAVER RHOEAS

COMMON NAMES: Corn Poppy, Shirley Poppy

The wrinkled paper-thin petals of this field flower pop open in vibrant shades of red, orange, pink, and yellow as well as white. As Dorothy and her friends discovered on their journey to Oz, poppies can produce a soothing, tranquilizing effect. The dried juice from the pods of one variety is used to create that potent anesthetic, known as opium.

CENTER

Roll a medium ball of light green dough into an oval. Insert a hooked 22g wire into one end. With needle tool, mark a line strongly around bead ⅓ of the way down from top. Indent center with umbrella tool and pinch 8 ridges in circle with bent nose tweezers. Insert 2-3 dozen fine black stamens ⅝"(16mm) long near base. Let dry. Paint ridges dark brown. Curve stamens upward.

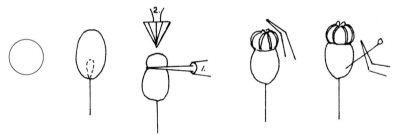

PETALS

Prepare mug with foil, making a shallow cup with a small hole in center. Roll an extra-small ball of red dough into a ring and place at edge of hole.

   Roll out red dough thin. Make cut with poppy or broad rose petal cutter. Press between corn husk veiners. Ruffle edge with paintbrush handle on edge of pad. Fold petal like an accordion for a moment. Open and attach to ring with glue. Repeat for second petal. Place opposite first in north-south position. Repeat process for third and fourth petals, placing east-west. Use fiber to lift petals slightly to form characteristic oval shape. Brush base of prepared center with glue and insert through petals. Press lightly to join. Let dry. Dust edges inward red.

   For pod, prepare center as above, omitting stamens. For leaves, use any shaggy leaf cutter with medium green dough. Dust center dark green and edge orange.

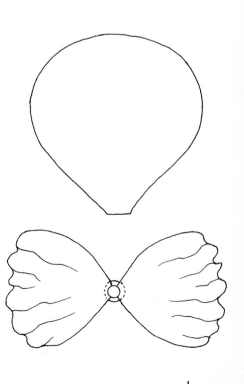

"Promising Love"

A couple of cattleyas are spotted snuggling atop this elegant engagement cake. Stephanotis, pulled blossoms, and variegated ivy show their support.

Stephanotis

The quintessential white wedding flower also appears in pink. Its tubular shape and delicate size make it an ideal choice for a groom's boutonniere or when building a bridal bouquet. It is formed without cutters using the pulled flower method.

METHOD

Roll a medium ball of dough into an "hourglass." Insert cone tool and make 5 cuts ⅜" (1cm) long around edge with exacto knife. Remove cone and open petals out. Gently pinch corners to round. To lengthen, pinch and pull petals outward.

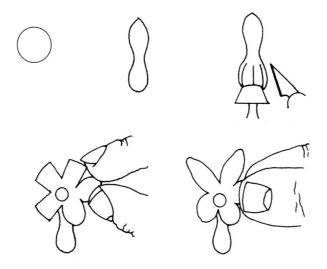

With needle tool, mark 1 or 2 lines down each petal. Insert hooked 26g wire through center. Hold upside down and with cuticle scissors, make 5 snips around base for calyx. Let dry. Dust center creamy yellow, back apple green and calyx dark green.

Clay pots and real stones can be used to display sugar creations that seem to be growing.

Sunflower

HELIANTHUS ANNUUS

State Flower of Kansas

This towering wildflower of late summer produces spectacular flower-heads that turn to face the sun as it traverses the heavens each day. Most often seen in bright yellow, other varieties blaze in shades of red and orange. For centuries, the common sunflower has been a symbol of the divine source of love and light.

CALYX

Form an extra-large ball of green dough into a Mexican Hat. Cut with large daisy cutter. On pad, thin edges with ball tool and point tips with needle tool. Insert a hooked 20g wire through center.

Roll out same dough thin and make second cut. Point tips and thin edges as before. Turn over and attach to base with glue, placing points in between those of first calyx.

PETALS (RAYS)

Roll out bright lemon yellow dough moderately thin. Cut with petal cutter. On pad, thin edge with ball tool. Insert a 28g wire ¾" (2cm) into base. On pad, draw 2 or 3 lines down petal using the side of the needle tool. Pinch tip with fingertips to point. Make at least 3 dozen. Let dry. Dust yellow orange up from base.

FLOWERHEAD

Roll out bright lemon yellow dough ¼" (7mm) thick. Cover with a 3" (7cm) square of tulle. Make cut with circular cutter 2" (5cm) wide. Use large ball tool in circular motion to slightly hollow out center. With needle tool, mark lines in center for starburst. Tease edges with needle tool. Dust hexing reddish brown and starburst black. Dip wires of 18 rays in glue and insert around edge, angled slightly upward. Insert second row of rays behind and in between first.

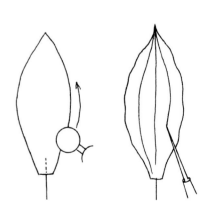

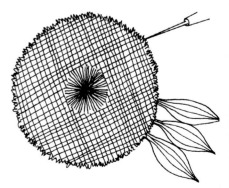

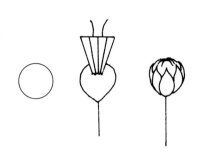

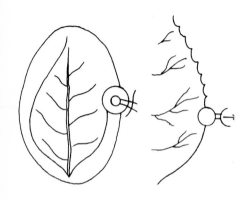

BUDS

Roll a medium ball of green dough into a stubby teardrop. Insert a hooked 28g wire into point. Indent with umbrella tool. Let dry. Make 2 or 3.

Roll out green dough thin and cut with small daisy cutter. Thin and point as with calyx. Brush glue in center and insert wire, wrapping around bud. Dust base dark green, edges burgundy.

LEAVES

Roll out green dough thin. Press with leaf veiner. Use leaf cutter or with circular blade, cut shape using template or freehand. On hard surface, mash out points around leaf using small ball tool for jagged edge. Thin edges with large ball tool on pad. Insert 26g wire into base. Shape with a slight curve. Make 5-9 of different sizes. Dust dark green down center and edges yellow orange.

ASSEMBLY

To finish flowerhead, roll out green dough moderately thin and cut with large daisy cutter. Texture as before. Brush center with glue, turn over and attach to prepared calyx. Brush glue on top and place back of flowerhead onto calyx to attach, pressing to secure. Let dry at least 24 hours.

For standing sunflower, tape 3 20g wires 12" (30cm) long to flower stem. Wrap leaf wires with tape to thicken. Attach leaves left and right down stem, tucking prepared buds at junctures. Dust stems yellowish green and burgundy at base of leaves.

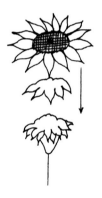

Guests will bask in your brilliance when you brighten up a party with this sunny "Sunflower Cake." Over fifty sugar petals radiate from the edge of a rounded cake over-piped with a grass tip.

Tuberose

POLIANTHES TUBEROSA

A heavenly scented summer bloomer with waxy white blossoms, the tuberose makes fabulous filler. Its jubilant trumpet flowers and buds cluster tightly at the tip of a long slender stem.

FLOWERS

Roll a large ball of dough into a long teardrop. Insert cone tool into wide end. With exacto knife, make 6 cuts ⅜" (1cm) long around edge. Remove cone and open petals out. Gently pinch corners to round. To lengthen, pinch and pull each petal outward.

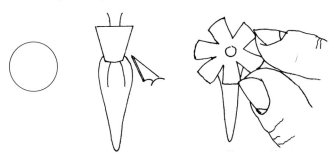

Place upside down on pad and thin petals with ball tool. With needle tool, mark lines inside edge of each petal. Slip a hooked 26g wire through center. Insert 6 apple green ministamens, tips protruding. Let dry. Dust center and base apple green. Make 3-5 per stem.

BUD

Roll a medium ball of dough into shape shown. With needle tool mark 3 creases down from tip. Insert 26g wire deeply into narrow end. Let dry. Dust apple green stronger than flowers. Make 3-5 per stem.

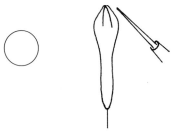

STEM

Wrap tape around the tip of a 22g wire and attach buds followed by open flowers, as in drawing. Dust tape apple green.

Water Lily

Nymphaea odorata

Throughout the ages, the water lily has inspired many artists with its graceful beauty. Floating in tranquil ponds, coves, and slow rivers from southern Canada to Florida's tip, it also finds a home in man-made water gardens. A sugar water lily with 27 unfolding petals is quite a mesmerizing centerpiece.

Center

Roll a medium ball of lemon yellow dough into a stubby tear-drop. Insert a hooked 22g wire into point. Indent other end with umbrella tool. Let dry

Roll out yellow dough thin and cut with small daisy cutter. With needle tool, draw line firmly down center of petals to point and curl. Insert base wire through center and attach with glue, curling over center. Repeat. Add a row using medium cutter and 2 more with large. Let dry. Dust tips orange.

Close-up of water lily.

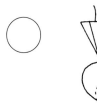

CALYX AND PETALS

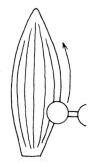

Cover mug with foil and make hole in center. Roll out green dough thin and press with lily leaf veiner. Make cut with petal cutter. Thin edges with ball tool on pad. No ruffles. Point tip with needle tool. Make 4 and place in cross around hole in foil.

For petals, make 9 with white dough and attach with glue in circle on calyx. Add 9 more and place in between first row, lifting with fiber. For third row of 9, use smaller cutter and attach in between second row, lifting tips higher. Brush glue under prepared center and insert through flower to join. Let dry. Dust tips of petals pink and pearlize.

LILY PAD

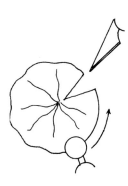

Roll out green dough thin and press with lily pad or nasturtium veiner. Cut with circular cutter and remove triangle with exacto knife. Ruffle edge with ball tool on pad. Let dry flat. Dust darker green and gloss with piping gel. Edge pink, red or orange. For water droplets, pipe with #2 tip using clear piping gel.

BUD

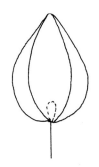

Roll a big ball of green dough into a softly pointed teardrop. Insert hooked 22g wire. With needle tool, mark 4 lines from tip to base. Dust dark green at base and red in creases, strongest at tip.

Pink Briar Rose on plaque.

Wild Rose

ROSA

COMMON NAME: Briar Rose

State Flower of New York

Blooming all summer long, this shrub brings forth 5-petaled flowers that open wide to reveal a sunny center. It is known for its sweet simplicity, like Sleeping Beauty, who was also named Briar Rose.

CENTER

Flatten a medium ball of yellow dough and press with tulle. Fold sides under to form stubby teardrop and insert hooked 22g wire. Tease edges with needle tool. Insert 36 yellow stamens ¾" (2cm) long around edge. Paint tips golden brown. Let dry. Dust center golden yellow.

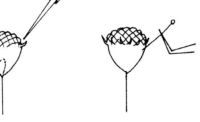

CALYX AND PETALS

Roll out green dough moderately thin and cut with calyx cutter. On pad, thin legs with ball tool and point tips with needle tool. Place in shallow former. Make hole in center.

Roll out dough thin and press with delicate veiner. Cut with large petal cutter. Softly ruffle edges on pad with ball tool. Brush glue on back of point and attach to calyx. Make 4 more and attach, overlapping. Brush bottom of prepared center with glue and insert wire through flower, pulling firmly. Let dry. Dust petals rose pink, leaving white circle around center.

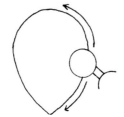

Vase of Anthuriums.

"The heart has its reasons which reason does not know."
BLAISE PASCAL

Anthurium

ANTHURIUM ANDREANUM

COMMON NAMES: Flamingo Plant, Painter's Palette, Pecker Plant

From spring until fall, this unusual flowering plant produces waxy heart-shaped leaves, called bracts. Its long protruding center or spadix bears minute flowers in a variety of colors. The broad, rippled bracts unfold in red, pink, orange, white, and even green.

SPADIX

For a large anthurium, roll an extra large ball of dough into a long tube with a wide end. Wrap with tulle to texture. Insert a hooked 20g wire into wide end. Curve slightly to dry. Dust spring green down from tip and middle lemon yellow.

BRACTS

Roll out red dough thick. Cut with heart cutter. Press with or sandwich between anthurium or orchid veiners. Thin edges with ball tool on pad for soft movement. Turn over and enhance point of heart with needle tool, drawing tool from tip to center. Brush glue on top near indentation. Place on fingers and insert spadix through dampened area. Press against bottom of spadix to secure and lay into large trumpet former. Lift spadix with fiber and curve point downward. Let dry. Dust bract deep red. Brush with loosened piping gel to gloss. To build stem, attach 2 or 3 long heavy wires with tape.

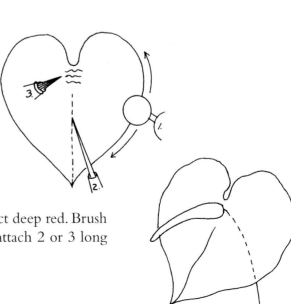

Bird of Paradise

STRELITZIA REGINAE

This extraordinary tropical flower is a native of South Africa and a member of the banana family. When the bright orange bracts and purple spearlike tongues emerge from the stalk, it resembles the head of a bird with a showy crest of colorful plumage. What an amazing and dramatic decoration!

TONGUE

Roll a large ball of dough into a pointed tube 3½" (9cm) long. On pad, mark crease ½" (13mm) from point with needle tool and draw line down center on both sides. Insert hooked 24g wire and dry with tip bending back.

Roll out blue dough thin and cut with elongated heart cutter. Thin edge with ball tool on pad and draw line down center with needle tool. Brush edge of tube below crease with glue and attach.

Roll out blue dough thin and cut with small rose petal cutter. Thin edges with ball tool and point rounded end with needle tool. Brush glue at point and wrap around tube right below heart. Let dry. Dust tip tan, heart and rest of tube violet. Dust rose petal blue.

Bird of Paradise on a plaque.

138

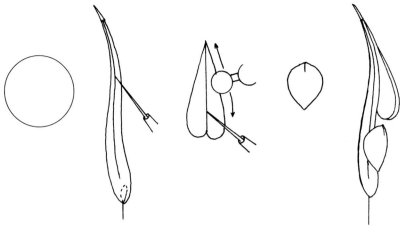

BRACTS

Roll out dough thin. Cut with lily petal cutter. Press between corn husk veiners and thin edge with ball tool on pad. With needle tool, draw line down center from tip to base and fold along crease. Brush inside of base with glue and attach to base of tongue opposite heart. Make 2 more and attach facing heart, overlapping each other.

Hint: When attaching, hang upside down and separate bracts and tongue with fiber.

Let dry. Dust bracts orange to yellow, leaving base white.

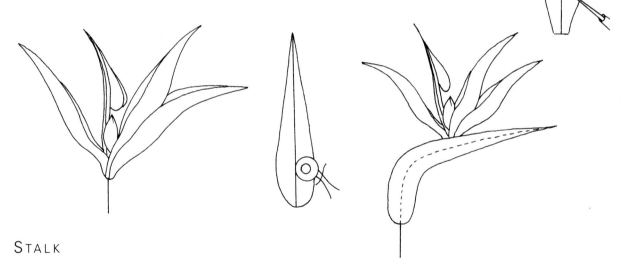

STALK

Start wrapping a 16-20g wire 8" (20cm) long with tape. Attach bract wire 4" (10cm) from tip. Bend main wire as shown.

To build stalk, roll a big ball of dough into a long pointed teardrop. With circular blade, cut in half. Brush each half with glue and attach below bracts, sandwiching wire. Let ½" (13mm) of main wire extend past dough. Mold into smooth round stalk.

Roll out large amount of green dough moderately thin. Cut a long narrow triangle 7" long by 2" wide (18cm x 5cm). Brush back with glue and wrap around previously molded dough. Dust upper edge red, sides and undersides dark green. Dust wire tip dark brown.

"EXPANDING COSMOS"

Bellflowers and cosmos explode from a sugar vase atop this imposing wedding cake. An even mixture of fondant and gum paste was used for bows and draping; royal icing panels forming the vase conceal the top tier.

Cosmos

COSMOS BIPINNATUS

Named from the Greek word meaning beautiful and harmonious universe, this early autumn flower expands across fields and gardens in white, pink, and crimson. The open flowers dance on spindly stems with thin, willowy leaves. A native of Mexico, it is well known for attracting butterflies and hummingbirds.

CENTER

Flatten a small ball of yellow dough and press with tulle. Tuck sides under and insert hooked 22g wire. Tease edges with needle tool. Insert 24 mini-yellow stamens ¼" (7mm) long around edge, angled up. Dust center golden yellow and paint stamen stems dark brown.

CALYX AND PETALS

Cover mug with foil. For calyx, roll out green dough thin and cut with small daisy cutter. Place on foil in mug and make hole in center with needle tool. For petals, roll out dough thin and cut with cosmos cutter. Thin edges on pad with ball tool. Mark 3-5 lines down petal with needle tool. Brush glue on back of base and attach to calyx. Make 3 more and attach to form cross. Make 4 more and place in between other petals. Brush glue under prepared center and insert wire through hole. Let dry. Dust greenish yellow near base of petals.

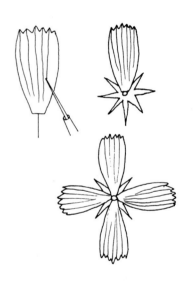

BUD

Roll a medium ball of dough into a stubby teardrop. Insert hooked 24g wire into wide end. Indent top with umbrella tool. Mark lines down sides with needle tool. Prepare calyx as before. Brush glue in center and insert bud wire to attach. Let dry. Dust center greenish yellow and tips of calyx pink.

LEAVES

Because of the delicate nature of its leaves, floral tape works best. For each stem, cut several long pointed strips of green tape. Stretch and attach middle to tip of green 28g wire. Continue down wire adding strips at ½" (13mm) intervals.

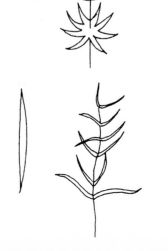

Gloriosa

GLORIOSA ROTHSCHILDIANA

COMMON NAMES: Flame Lily, Glory Lily, Climbing Lily

Similar in structure to a shuttlecock, the green petals of this magnificent flower slowly bend backward and then burst into flaming colors as they mature. A marvel of nature, this climbing vine was first discovered in southern Africa. The technique of layering different colored doughs described here achieves the characteristic contrast of vibrant red and yellow.

STIGMA AND OVARY

Make 2 snips ½" (13mm) long in a 3" (7cm) strip of green floral tape. With index finger and thumb, twist each snip into a thread. Continue down tape 2" (5cm) to form stigma. Place a 22g wire inside remaining tape and twist to connect. At tip of wire, bend stigma 90°.

Three Flame Lilies.

For ovary, roll a small ball of light green dough into a bead. Insert the wire through bead and brush glue below bend to attach. With needle tool, mark 3 lines around bead. Gloss with piping gel loosened with water. Let dry.

STAMENS

Roll a tiny ball of light green dough into a tube ½" (13mm) long. Insert the tip of a 24g wire into middle and pinch to connect. With needle tool, mark line across top. Let dry. Brush sides only with glue and dip into orange pollen mixture. Leave center line green. Make 6 per flower.

PETALS

Roll out deep red dough thin. Make cut with lily petal cutter. Cover to prevent drying. Roll out bright yellow dough moderately thin. Place red piece on top of yellow dough and roll out to join layers. Place cutter below red point leaving a "V" of yellow at the base. With ball tool, thin and softly ruffle edges on pad. Insert 28g wire into base. With needle tool, point petal and mark line down center. Fold in half and curve tip backward to dry on flat surface. Make 6. Brush inside with piping gel loosened with water. Let dry. Dust back red, leaving yellow "V" and lightly at base spring green.

Hint: To vary the size of flower, use a circular blade to cut out the simple shape of the petal.

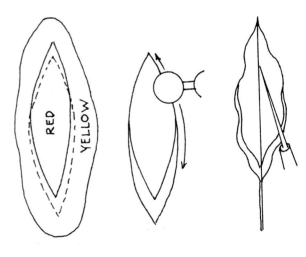

ASSEMBLY

Attach green floral tape to prepared wire just below ovary. Wrap stamens in a circle to wire leaving 1½" (4cm) lengths. Attach petals below stamens, ruffles facing center. Bend main wire 90° near center and bend petals backward, as in drawing.

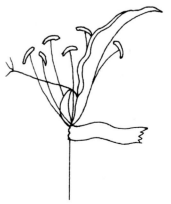

Close-up of fall flowers with spider mum on lower right.

Spider Mum

CHRYSANTHEMUM

The mum family spans over 160 species including the common daisy, with flowers ranging in size from an inch to six inches (25mm–15cm) in diameter. Originally from Asia, their exquisite symmetry has adorned Oriental tapestries and paintings for centuries. The variety called spider mum spins long threadlike petals in a broad range of colors.

CENTER

Flatten a medium ball of yellow dough and press with tulle. Fold sides under and insert a hooked 24g wire. Let dry. Dust surface apple green and edges rust.

PETALS

Roll out red-orange dough thin and cut with smallest of 3 daisy cutters. (If petals are wide, cut in half with exacto knife.) With needle tool, start past tip and draw line down center firmly, pointing and curving petals upward. Brush glue in center and halfway down each petal. Insert wire through center, wrapping petals around base. Repeat for second cut. Add 2 rows with medium cutter and 2 with large. (Vary number of rows for different size flowers.)

For calyx, use green dough and cut with small daisy cutter. Attach to back of flower with glue.

When you show your mummy, mum's the word it's sugar!

*"Deep in their roots,
all flowers keep the light."*
THEODORE ROETHKE

Cattleya Orchid

One of the largest members of the orchid family, this showy exotic is a classic choice for corsages and wedding bouquets. The "Queen of Orchids" is dressed in a rich array of flamboyant colors such as magenta, saffron, and tangerine as well as softer shades of lavender and pink.

TONGUE

Roll a medium ball of dough into a long teardrop. With ball tool, hollow out center. Hook and curve a 24g wire and insert into point. Pinch other end with tweezers and snip sides with curved scissors. Let dry. Dust snips pink and hollow yellow.

*A single sugar orchid
makes any cake quite special.*

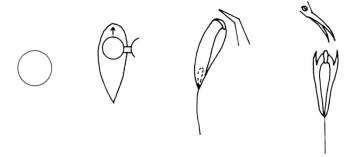

THROAT

Roll out dough moderately thin and press with orchid veiner. Make cut with throat cutter. With friller tool, distress outer edge. Strongly ruffle with narrow dowel, rolling back and forth on pad near edge of table. For pollen tracts, pinch 5 lines with tweezers as shown. Brush glue below tracts and attach tongue. Fold sides of throat around tongue. Let dry on fiber with ruffles curving down. Dust tracts yellow and ruffles and edges pink.

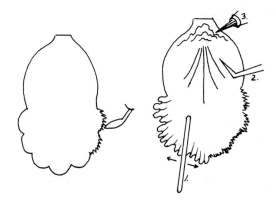

SEPALS

Roll out dough moderately thin and press with corn husk veiner. Make cut with sepal cutter. On pad, thin edges with ball tool. With needle tool, draw line lightly down back of petal. Insert 28g wire into base. Fold softly in half and place on fiber to shape. Make 3 and let dry. Dust base apple green and edges violet.

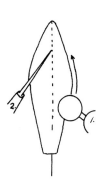

SIDE PETALS

Roll out pale violet dough thin and press with orchid veiner. Cut with petal cutter. Ruffle edge as with throat but do *not* distress edge. With needle tool, draw line down back of petal. Insert 28g wire into base and fold softly in half. Let dry on fiber to shape. Make 2. Dust edges pink and violet.

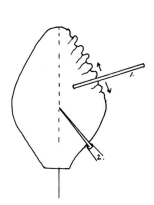

ASSEMBLY

Wrap tape to wire at base of throat and attach left and right petals. Join sepals in a triangular fashion. Pearlize entire flower for waxy texture.

Christmas rose, holly, and mistletoe on plaque.

Christmas Rose

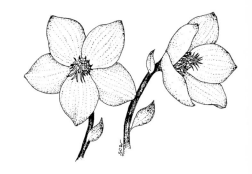

HELLEBOROUS NIGER

According to folklore, this flower grew in the garden of heaven and was tended by the angels, who called it the "Rose of Love." Archangel Gabriel brought it to earth by merely touching the frozen ground to announce the birth of the Christ child. The waxy white sepals surround a creamy yellow center on a mahogany-colored stem.

CENTER

Flatten a medium ball of cream dough and texture with tulle. Fold sides under to form stubby teardrop and insert a hooked 22g wire. With cuticle scissors, snip points around edge. Indent center with umbrella tool and insert 12 white mini-stamens without tips ⅜" (1cm) long. Let dry. Dust snips apple green.

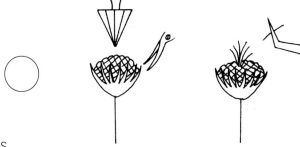

SEPALS

Roll out dough moderately thin and press with delicate veiner. Make cut with stubby rose petal cutter. With ball tool, thin edges on pad and softly point tip with needle tool. Insert 30g wire. In palm, cup with ball tool. Make 5 and let dry. Dust base apple green and pearlize.
    Variation: Dust edges and back pale pink.

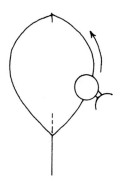

ASSEMBLY

Attach tape to wire under center and join sepal wires to main stem, overlapping. Dust stem reddish-brown for woody appearance.

*"Beauty is not caused.
It is."*

EMILY DICKINSON

Cymbidium Orchid

This large exotic beauty bursts into bloom in hundreds of different shades, from pastel to the most vibrant colors. On most varieties, the throat and tongue are boldly speckled with burgundy. Making a gorgeous *cymbidium* is truly a rewarding experience.

TONGUE

Roll a medium ball of dough into a 1" (25mm) tube. Curve a 22g wire and insert into one end. Indent other end with #7 tip and divide in half with needle tool. Pinch thin flaps on sides like a cobra's hood and curve forward. Let dry. Dust back of hood pink, leaving circle white. With detail brush, paint burgundy dots.

Left, a fantasy stem of cymbidium orchids explores various color possibilities. Above, a luscious cymbidium orchid resting on a bed of roses elaborates this charming christening cake.

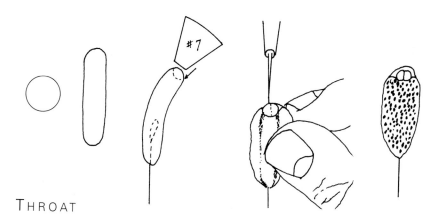

THROAT

Roll out dough moderately thin and make cut with throat cutter. Ruffle scalloped area on pad with ball tool; thin and cup sides. Brush with glue and wrap a round bottom of tongue. Curve ruffle downward to dry.

For pollen tracts, roll 2 tiny pieces of dough into pointed tubes and attach with glue under tongue. Brush tracts with glue and sprinkle with yellow pollen mixture. With detail brush, paint speckles on ruffle with burgundy and dust edges pink.

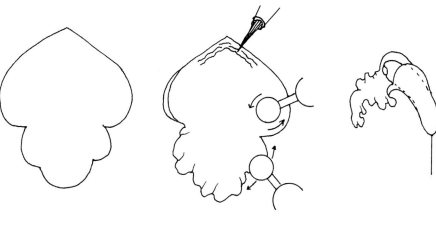

SEPALS AND PETALS

Cover mug with foil and make hole in center. Roll out dough thin and press with lily leaf veiner. Cut with sepal cutter. Thin edges with ball tool and point tip with needle tool. Place at edge of hole. Curve tip forward with fiber. Make 2 more and place in triangle, attaching bottoms with glue.

For 2 side petals, repeat process as above with slightly larger cutter. Attach with glue and place between sepals at 10 and 2 o'clock. Lift with fiber. Brush bottom of throat with glue and insert through hole. Prop throat with fiber. Let dry 24 hours. Dust base of petals pink and pearlize.

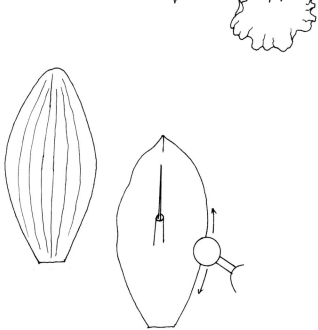

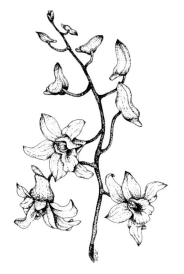

Dendrobium Orchid

COMMON NAME: Singapore Orchid

Deriving its name from the Greek words *dendron* and *bios*, meaning "tree of life," this miniature orchid originated in the tropical climates of Asia. Its popularity has led to cultivation in hothouses all over the world. Graduating sizes of open flowers to buds on a delicate stem make it a favorite for wedding bouquets. *Dendrobiums* create a lovely trailing effect in white, pinks, and purples.

TONGUE

Roll a small ball of dough into a ½" (13mm) tube. Curve a hooked 24g wire and insert into one end. Indent other end with #5 tip and with needle tool, divide circle in half. Pinch thin flaps on sides like a cobra's hood and curve forward. Let dry. Dust back and edges pink. Leave circle white.

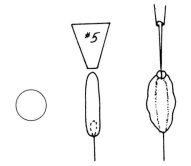

*Dendrobium orchids
with lunaria seed pods
shining below.*

THROAT

Roll out dough moderately thin and cut with throat cutter. With ball tool, thin edges on pad. With tweezers, pinch 3 ridges for pollen tracts. Brush glue below tracts and wrap sides around base of tongue to attach. Curve ruffle downward to dry. Dust ridges yellow and edges pink.

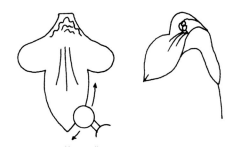

SIDE PETALS

Roll out dough thin and cut side petals. Thin edges with ball tool and point tip with needle tool. Brush glue at base and attach to side of throat. Repeat for other side. Let dry.

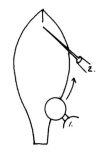

SEPALS

Roll out dough thin and make cut with sepal cutter. Thin edges and point tip as above. Insert throat wire through center and attach with glue, curving back to dry. Dust all tips and edges pink or mauve. Pearlize.

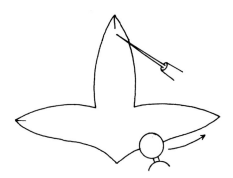  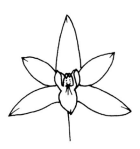

BUDS

Form dough into a "hen" shape. Mark lines with needle tool as shown. Insert a hooked 24g wire into belly. Let dry. Make 5-7 gradually increasing in size. Dust ends pink and middle apple green.

ASSEMBLY

Attach tape to tip of a 22g wire and wrap smallest bud. Travel down wire adding buds and flowers in increasing sizes. Dust stem medium green and pink at junctures.

Oncidium Orchid

COMMON NAMES: Dancing Ladies, Golden Shower

With its tigerish stripes, this native of the tropics showers miniature golden flowers from delicate emerald stems. The open orchid resembles a figure with outstretched arms and widespread skirt, bringing to mind a "dancing lady." A branch of *oncidiums* makes a delightful airy background for larger flowers.

*Festive orchids
dance in the air above
a simple bud vase.*

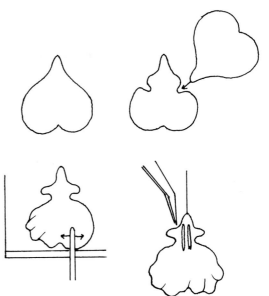

FORMING THROAT

Roll out bright yellow dough on a slope from thick to thin. Cut with small heart-shaped cutter with point over thick end. Cut out 2 indentations as shown with point of cutter. With ball tool, work out "arms" and thin all edges but tip. On edge of pad, roll toothpick or paintbrush handle back and forth to make tiny ruffles around "skirt." Insert damp 24g wire into point. With tweezers, pinch pollen tracts left and right of wire. Let dry.

ADDING SEPALS

Form a very tiny Mexican Hat with same dough. Cut with narrow 5-pointed calyx cutter. On pad, thin "legs" with small ball tool. With tiny ball tool, indent hole as shown. Bend throat wire near point and brush with glue. Insert into hat under hole to join. Let dry.

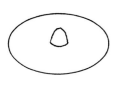

BUDS

Roll a small ball of same dough into a teardrop. Insert damp 30g wire into wide end. Rotate and work dough to wire. Insert point into rounded cuticle scissors and make 3 shallow snips around bud. Let dry. Make at least 5 in decreasing sizes.

PAINTING AND ASSEMBLY

Dust all edges and tips golden yellow. With detail brush, paint intermittent stripes down sepals, on buds and open flowers with rich reddish-brown food color. Paint spots around pollen tracts. Pearlize lightly.

   To assemble, attach smallest bud to tip of a 24g wire with floral tape. Travel down wire and attach buds in increasing sizes followed by open flowers. Dust stems emerald green.

Phalaenopsis Orchid

COMMON NAMES: Moth Orchid, Butterfly Orchid

As its common names suggest, this tropical beauty opens broad winglike petals when mature. Their rounded shape lends a soft feminine quality to any arrangement. These orchids appear in unlimited color variations. Described here is a classic white orchid with yellow and pink accents in its delicate center.

"BAMBOOZLED"
Sleight-of-hand turns sugar dough into natural and ebony bamboos in this sweet illusion of moth orchids in a planter.

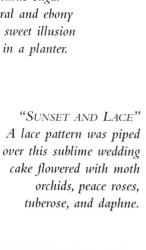

"SUNSET AND LACE"
A lace pattern was piped over this sublime wedding cake flowered with moth orchids, peace roses, tuberose, and daphne.

TONGUE

Curve a hooked 24g wire. Roll a small ball of dough into a long pointed bead. Draw line down center with needle tool. With tweezers, pinch a ridge on either side of bead at one end. Curve into "C" shape and insert wire. Indent #3 tip to form "eyes." Let dry. Dust golden yellow in center. Paint tiny pink dots on ridges.

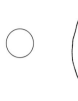 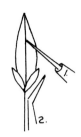  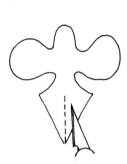

THROAT

Roll out dough moderately thin and make cut with throat cutter. With exacto knife, split point to form "legs." With ball tool, thin and lengthen legs on pad. With needle tool, curl legs by drawing line down center. Thin other edges with ball tool and cup "head" and "arms" in palm. Brush glue on back of tongue and insert wire above center as shown. Let dry. Dust curled tips and edges pink.

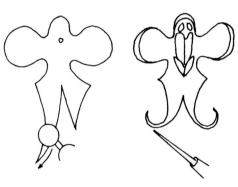

SEPALS

Prepare mug or wide-mouth glass with shallow foil. Make hole in center. Roll out dough thin and make cut with sepal cutter. Press with lily leaf veiner. On pad, thin edges with ball tool. Turn over. With needle tool, lightly draw line down center of each sepal and softly fold in half. Place in mug.

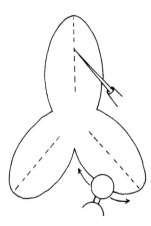

PETALS

Roll out dough moderately thin and cut out 2 side petals. Press with delicate veiner. Thin edges with ball tool on pad. On back, draw line lightly down center with needle tool. Attach each petal to center of sepals with glue. Lift with fiber to shape. Brush back of throat with glue and insert wire through center. Let dry. Dust base of each petal creamy yellow and then pearlize for waxy texture.

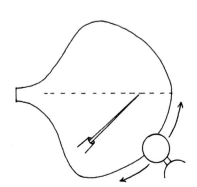

BUD

Roll a large ball of dough into a stubby teardrop. Insert a hooked 22g wire into bottom. With needle tool, draw 3 lines from tip to base. Let dry. Dust base apple green and tip pink. Pearlize.

"Star light, star bright,
First star I see tonight.
I wish I may, I wish I might,
Have this wish I wish tonight."
Children's Verse

Poinsettia

EUPHORBIA PULCHERRIMA

The leaves of this deciduous shrub from Central America are often mistakenly thought to be the petals of the flower. Actually, the tiny bead-shaped flowers are clustered at the center of radiating white, pink, or red uneven leaves called "bracts." Pots of poinsettia pop up everywhere every year to brighten the winter holiday season.

"WINTER WEDDING"
Snowy poinsettias top a grand basket made of three stacked cakes. Gum paste rings and placard were painted with nontoxic gold powder.

158

PREPARING BRACTS

For a white poinsettia, roll out light cream dough moderately thin. Press with leaf veiner and cut with large poinsettia or lily cutter. Thin edges with ball tool. Do *not* ruffle. Insert a damp 26g wire. Fold in half, then open and let dry flat. Make 5 with cream dough and at least 3 with medium green for background.

With cream dough, make 5 more bracts using medium cutter and 28g wires and 3 using smallest cutter and 30g wires. Let dry. Dust all cream bracts apple green down center vein, stronger at base. Dust green ones darker green and edge red.

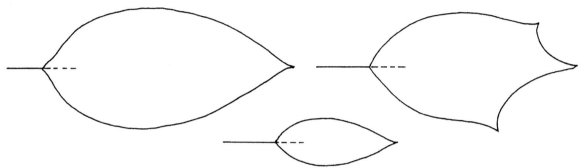

FLOWERS

Roll an extra-small ball of green dough into a teardrop. Insert a damp 30g green wire into point. Indent wide end with tip of umbrella tool. With curved cuticle scissors, make at least 5 snips around shape. Make 4 and 5 more with yellow dough. Let dry. Dust all medium green at base. With detail brush, paint edge of indentation and tips of snips with bright red food color.

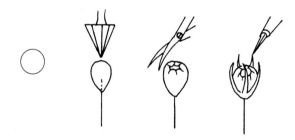

ASSEMBLY

With green floral tape, join 3 flowers to the tip of a 24g wire. Bend wire of smallest bract 90° and attach below flowers. Build 3 clusters in this way. Join together with floral tape, forming a single stem with bracts pointing out. Join 5 medium bracts in a circle around stem. Then add 5 large cream bracts, followed by 3 or more green ones.

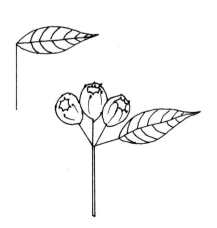

VARIATIONS

For a pink poinsettia, use cream dough. Dust base of bracts apple green and center and edges pink.

For red, use red dough and dust deep red, followed by violet at base and edges.

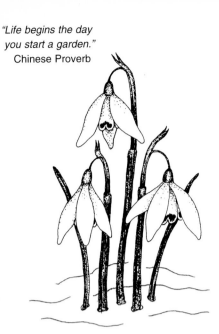

Snowdrop

GALANTHUS NIVALIS

COMMON NAMES: Fair Maid of February, Milk Flower, *Perce-neige* (Piercing Snow)

How generous is the melting snow to offer us this hardy little flower as a promise of spring's arrival! Its drooping milky white petals with emerald accents dangle from canelike stems, surrounded by long thin leaves.

Drooping snowdrops and a small bird clutching a withered branch share a snowy mound of cake. White icing dusted with powdered sugar was sprinkled with edible glitter for a frosty look.

INNER PETALS

Roll an extra-small ball of dough into a teardrop. Dip a cone tool into cornstarch and insert into round end. With exacto blade, make 3 cuts ¼" (7mm) long around dough. Remove tool and spread sections out. Round corners with fingertips. With tiny scissors, snip a triangle out of the middle of each petal. Place on pad. With small ball tool *inside*, roll each petal into a heart shape. Pull a hooked 28g wire through center until it is concealed. Round petals. Let dry. Dust top of each petal apple green. With emerald food color, paint an inverted heart around snip. Leave edge white.

OUTER PETALS

Roll out dough thin and cut with narrow 3-petaled cutter. With ball tool, thin edges on pad. Then roll down middle of petal toward center to cup and curve. Insert prepared wire through center and attach with glue. Hang to dry. Dust very top apple green.

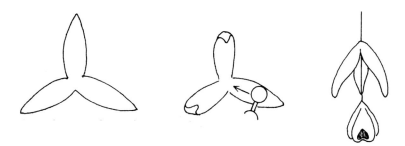

CAP, STEM, AND LEAVES

Roll a tiny ball of bright green dough into a bead. With small ball tool, indent one side. Insert wire through center and attach above petals with glue. Glaze with piping gel.

For stem, roll a small ball of bright green dough into a long thin pointed tube. Make snip in point ⅛" (4mm) long. With needle tool, mark line down tube. Brush line with glue and attach to flower wire, extending past cap. Bend flower downward.

For leaves, roll out thin tube of same dough and texture with corn husk or veiner. Insert a 24g wire into base. Mark strong line down center with needle tool. Curve slightly to dry. Dust with dark green and glaze with piping gel. Edge golden yellow.

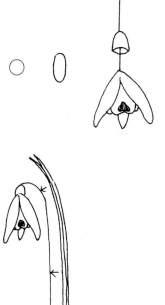

PART THREE

❖ ❖ ❖

A Gallery of Cakes

Birthdays
Children

"HONEY BEAR"
*Sugar bees buzz about a brave
little bear sidetracked on his way to
a birthday bash.*

*Left, claws are out for the nectar
in the hive!*

"HIS FIRST SHOE"
For birthday or baby shower,
an oversized shoe cake fits the
occasion.

"PAMPERED PUP"
Children of any age rejoice
at seeing their beloved pet
immortalized in cake like this
adoring Maltese.

"KOOKY COOKIE MONSTER"
Look who got his paws into Jared's cookie jar!

"BIG BIRD BIRTHDAY"
Left, bright feathers piped with a leaf tip bring to
life a favorite Sesame Street character.

"PETER'S CARROT PATCH"
A child's favorite book can inspire an endearing birthday cake. This creation marked the 100th anniversary
of Beatrix Potter's classic tale.

Teen Birthday

"HEARTS AND FLOWERS"
A stunning stargazer steals focus on a lacy "Sweet 16" cake.

"DOWN THE SLOPES!"
A larger-than-life sport shoe cake is an amusing choice for all ages.

Adult Birthday

"King of Hearts"
A king-sized deck of cards
suits the game enthusiast.
Ante up sugar poker chips!

"Victory Day"
Extra! Extra! Read all about it!
Deliver a newspaper cake with
personalized copy for any
special event and get rave reviews.

"Preserving the Mariner"
Toss a life preserver cake to a
serious sailing buff.

"Moroccan Sunburst"
Gum paste tiles colored like
malachite form a mosaic pattern
on a hexagonal canister cake.

Shower and Engagement

"STARRY NIGHT"
On this romantic engagement cake, floodwork panels form a container bursting with a kaleidoscope of flowers and berries.

"BABY BOTTLE BLUE"
Expectant mothers will be tickled pink, or blue, receiving a larger-than-life nurser in cake.

"SHOWERS OF HAPPINESS"
Floodwork and gum paste techniques were combined for a shopping bag cake stuffed with gifts and flowers for the bride-to-be.

Wedding

"A Dream Come True"

Inspired by the classical beauty of ancient Greece, this majestic wedding cake points us heavenward. A square base softly draped with sugar dough rises to an octagon, eight columns, and a dome-shaped top tier. Top left, close-up of dome. Bottom left, wires dotted with royal icing gush from sugar urns filled with miniature roses and star flowers.

"Aspiring Love"
A wedding cake, the centerpiece of the reception, can create treasured memories that last a lifetime.

"Knife Spray"
Make the cake-cutting ceremony even more special by dressing up the knife with matching sugar flowers.

"Orchids upon Orchids"
Dendrobiums and ivy swirl around large spotted cattleyas.

"ROYAL AFFAIR"
Sugar petals are strewn beneath double-decker tiers of this palatial design.

"BRIDAL PARTY"
Nine blushing bouquets
congregate around a
grand wedding cake.

"FANCY FREE"
A flowery top tier drops blossoms and buds below, lending
a less formal air to this traditional design.

"BASKETS ABLOOM"
Three basket tiers brim over
with piped flowers, complemented
by sculpted sweet violets, ivy, and
leaves.

"SOMETHING BLUE"
Graceful sugar draping hangs loosely
around bud roses and huge Casablanca
lilies atop this two-tier wedding cake.

"Champagne Wishes"
A toast to the happy couple
with a basket full of beauty.

"Wedding Book"
A pair of cakes were wed
to form an unconventional
design strewn with gerber
daisies, mums, bittersweet,
and acorns in vibrant
fall colors.

"Cathedral in the Clouds"
Inspired by the majestic Russian cathedral at Zagorsk, this architectural wedding cake design appears to ascend as an impressive cloud formation.

"Loving Cup"
A wooden pedestal covered with fondant supports a massive urn cake, which runneth over with roses, sweet peas, freesia, and ivy.

"DEARLY BELOVED"
Fans of gum paste pleats flock behind jubilant lilies that "are gathered here today."

"AUTUMN LACE"
A pattern of piped grapes patted flat mirrors the shape of the pearlized pods on top.

Anniversary

"POODLES PRESENT"
An anniversary gift cake is sweetened by the presence of a beloved pair of tea-cup poodles. As keepsakes, doggies were sculpted in Styrofoam and piped with royal icing; details are gum paste.

"RUBY ANNIVERSARY"
Forty years of togetherness are celebrated with a monogrammed jewelry box studded with red sugar gems.

"Earning the Gold"
A sugar urn rests upon
a pedestal of square
cakes for a fiftieth wedding
anniversary celebration

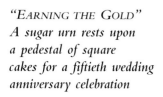

Holidays

Easter

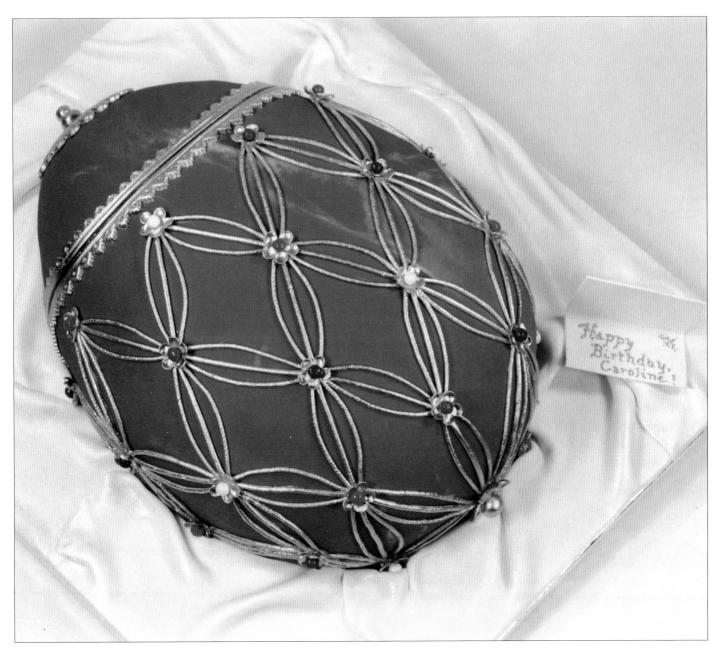

"ABSOLUTELY FABERGÉ"

In the style of the renowned Russian artist, this marbleized egg cake, nesting in folds of satiny fondant, is hatched with golden mesh and sugar gems.

Mother's Day

"MOTHER EARTH"
This tribute to motherhood transports us to a grassy knoll where a bird's nest harbors new life.

Right, close-up of nest. A "Clouded Yellow" Butterfly peeks in on the eggs while mother bird is away.

Father's Day

"Puttin' on the Ritz"
Most of the decorations on this Floridian golf course cake are painted floodwork stood upright on toothpicks attached with royal icing.

Right, the versatility of gum paste as a sculpting medium is shown here with stones, cattails, bowed bridge, and gaping gator.

Graduation Day

"GRADUATION DAY"
Sweeten commencements with a fondant-covered cake topped with a sugar mortarboard and tassel. What a capital idea when honoring the scholastic achiever!

Winter Holiday

"DECK THE HALLS!"
For a delightful wreath cake centerpiece, pipe green icing leaves around a ring of cake and dot with gum paste berries and a bow.

"FESTIVE ORNAMENT"
An old-fashioned bauble cake ornately trimmed with royal icing filigree.

"IN COMES COMPANY"
Any company's logo can be reproduced easily using floodwork techniques. This cake was for Stephen Sondheim and the cast of the 1995 Broadway revival.

"ARCHITECTURAL DIGESTION"
Building cakes are a common request for cake artists. Royal icing captures in sharp detail this design by I.M. Pei and Associates planned for Boston harbor.

"Cake Double"
Products duplicated in cake, like this elegant perfume bottle, always make a splash at corporate events.

PART FOUR

Other Sugar Decorations

MORE GEMS OF NATURE

ACORN	GRAPES
BITTERSWEET	IVY
BUMBLEBEE	LADYBUG
BUTTERFLY	LUNARIA
CATTAIL	MISTLETOE
DRAGONFLY	MUSHROOM
ENGLISH HOLLY	PUSSY WILLOW
FIDDLEHEAD FERN	WHEAT

A c o r n

In September, the grounds beneath the mighty oak are strewn with this tiny fruit. Because there are numerous varieties of oak trees, size, shape, and color of acorns vary greatly. Described here is just one of the many possibilities.

NUT

Roll an extra-large ball of light green dough into a wide bead. Insert a hooked wire into one end. Indent other end with a #5 tip. Let dry. Paint streaks lengthwise on sides with brown piping gel, leaving tip green.

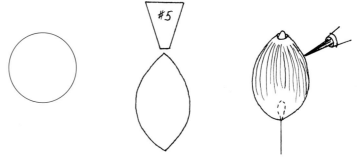

CAP

Flatten a medium ball of golden brown dough. Texture one side with tulle. Insert nut wire through center and attach with glue. With needle tool, tease edge of cap to join to nut. Dust cap and tip of nut brown.

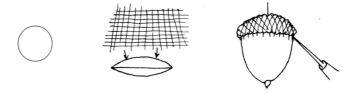

FALL OAK LEAF

Roll out golden brown dough moderately thin. Press with leaf veiner and cut with oak leaf cutter. Thin edges with ball tool on pad and insert 26g wire. Let dry on polyester to shape. Dust reddish-brown. Gloss with piping gel.

Bittersweet

CELASTRUS SCANDENS

The brilliant colors of autumn are displayed by this woody vine with its clusters of tiny amber and scarlet fruits. As the berries mature, the seed covers burst open, exposing the shiny red flesh. Branches of bittersweet are a festive addition to any fall arrangement.

BERRIES

Form an extra-small ball of golden yellow dough. Insert 30g wire. Let dry. Glaze with piping gel. With detail brush, paint a tiny brown dot opposite wire. Make at least 5 per cluster.

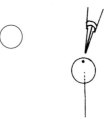

OPEN FRUIT

Form an extra-small ball of red dough. Insert 30g wire. With needle tool, mark 5 lines as shown. Let dry. Glaze.

For hull, roll out golden yellow dough thin. Cut with small rounded 5-petal cutter. Cup each section with ball tool and point with needle tool. Insert red berry wire through center and attach with glue to back of berry. Bend backward *or* close around berry for variation. Let dry. Make at least 3 per cluster.

ASSEMBLY

With floral tape, attach berries unevenly down a 24g wire. Dust stem reddish-brown.

Close-up of bumblebee.

Bumblebee

*"Fairy places, fairy things,
Fairy woods where the wild bee wings."*
R.L. Stevenson

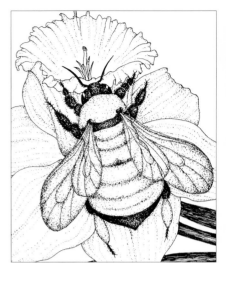

Bombus

Common Name: Humblebee

A chubby little bee with its black and yellow stripes can add a comical touch of Nature. Bring a work of art to life with a humble bumblebee. When "Sweet Eden" was displayed, one wedding guest spent half the reception trying to shoo the sugar bee off the cake!

Wings

Make template of shape shown. Roll out cream dough moderately thin and cut out with exacto knife. Flip template for second wing. Thin edges with ball tool on pad and insert 30g wire ⅜" (1cm) long into point. With detail brush, paint brown veins. Let dry. Pearlize.

Legs

Roll a tiny ball of yellow dough into a bead. Thread onto black stamen stem ¾" (2cm) long. Make 2 for back "pollen sacks." For 2 middle legs, divide bead in half with needle tool and, for front, into thirds. Curve and let dry.

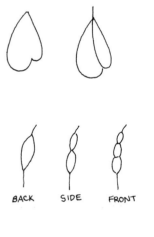

BACK SIDE FRONT

Body

Form a large ball of yellow dough into shape shown. Indent with #10 tip for head. Indent #6 tip twice for eyes. With needle tool, mark lines as shown. Hook and curve a 24g wire and insert into belly. Brush wings and legs with glue and insert. Insert 2 black stamen stems ¼" (7mm) long above eyes for antennae. Let dry.

Coloring Bee

For yellow areas, brush with glue and sprinkle with yellow pollen mixture, including back legs. Paint the remaining sections black, including a small triangle between wings.

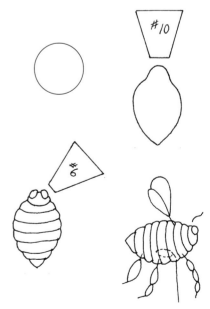

B·U·Z·Z·Z·Z·Z·Z·z·z·z·Z·z·z· · · · ·

Butterfly

LEPIDOPTERA

The name "butterfly" comes from the Old French word *biaute*, meaning beauty, which certainly applies to this exquisite creature. English folklore held the notion that this "fly" was notorious for stealing milk and butter. It also may have been inspired by the common butter-colored variety, like the Clouded Yellow (*Colias crocea*), described here. What could be more stunning than a lifelike sugar butterfly landing on your creation!

"SUNNING APOLLOS"

Various violets grow at the foot of a tree stump cake. The caterpillar in the foreground, called Apollo, matures into its adult form, a dramatic red-spotted butterfly.

WINGS

Roll out lemon yellow dough moderately thin. Using template or cutter, cut out left and right wings. Thin edges on pad, except for point. Insert a 30g wire ⅜" (1cm) long into point. With needle tool, draw subtle line. Let dry. With detail brush, paint edges, veins, and markings black. Dust out from base orange.

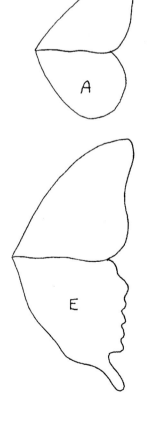

BODY

Roll a medium ball of black dough into shape shown. With needle tool, mark lines in abdomen and insert #3 tip for eyes. Make snip below eyes for mouth. Bend 22g wire 2" (5cm) long and insert into belly. Set in Styrofoam.

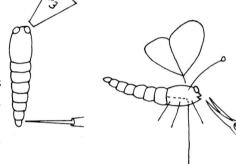

For legs, insert 6 black stamen stems ½" (13mm) into thorax as shown. Brush glue on wing wires and insert into sides. Prop up with wooden blocks (or spice tins). Insert 2 curved stamens 1" (25mm) above eyes for antennae. Let dry. Brush abdomen with glue and sprinkle with gelatin for fuzzy texture.

This is one butterfly that didn't need a cocoon!

OTHER WING PATTERNS

A – SATYR B – APOLLO C – CLEOPATRA D – NYMPH
E – PASHA F – SWALLOWTAIL G – MONARCH H – SKIPPER

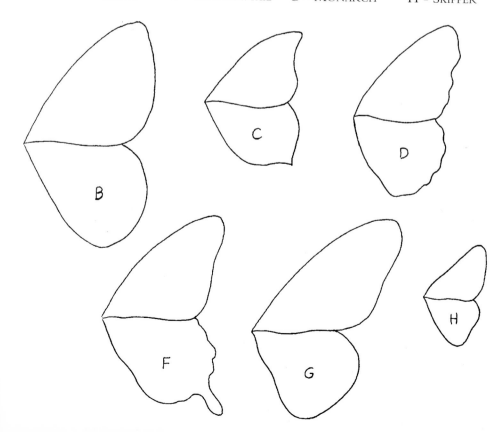

"NATURE'S BOUNTY"

Colorful lilies of the field abound in a dark chocolate wicker basket, the stunning centerpiece of a summer wedding.

Cattail

Typha

COMMON NAME: Reed Mace

From May through July, cattails stand tall overlooking ponds and marshes. Their minute flowers form a fuzzy, reddish-brown spike like the tail of a cat. Easy to make, they are wonderful filler for arrangements of wildflowers.

FORMATION

Roll a ball of apple green dough into a tube. Insert a long wire deeply into one end. Work dough to wire. Insert a short length of green wire or stamen thread into other end. Let dry. Dust reddish-brown, stronger at ends.

Note: Depending on desired size of cattail, from miniature to extra-large, choose an appropriate gauge of wire to support it.

REEDS

Roll out light green dough moderately thin and press with corn husk or veiner. With circular blade, cut long thin triangular shape. Thin edges with ball tool. Brush glue down lower half and wrap around cattail stem. Bend upper half down. Let dry. Dust stem and reed darker green and edge red.

Close-up of dragonfly.

Dragonfly

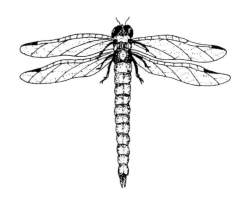

O*DONATA*

C*OMMON* N*AMES:* Darning Needle, Devil's Darning Needle

For eons, the dragonfly's form has remained unchanged and has therefore become a symbol of eternal life. Its long narrow body and filmy airplanelike wings enable it to dart quickly and smoothly across land and water. Its iridescent blue, green, or brown coloring flashes in the sunlight.

W*INGS*

Roll out dough thin. With exacto blade, cut 2 of each wing template. Insert 30g wire, ¼" (7mm) long into each bottom. Let dry. With detail brush, paint edges, veins and accent dots with dark blue food color. Brush with blue lustre dust.

B*ODY*

Roll a large ball of blue dough into a tube 2" (5cm) long with a wide end. Indent #5 tip left and right for eyes. With scissors, make tiny snip vertically below eyes. With needle tool, mark head and body lines as shown. Insert a bent 22g wire into belly. Place in Styrofoam and lift abdomen with fiber. Insert 6 black stamen stems ½"(13mm) long into thorax for legs and 2 stems ¼" (7mm) long on sides of mouth. Insert wings into thorax as shown, parallel to Styrofoam. Let dry. Paint eyes with dark brown piping gel and body segments dark blue. Brush body with blue lustre dust.

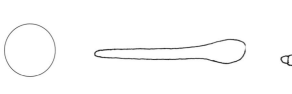

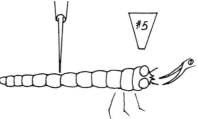

"Deck the halls with boughs of holly!
Fa la la la la la la la la!"
Old English Carol

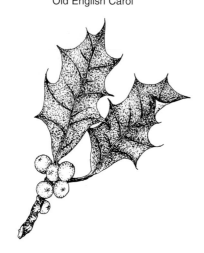

English Holly

ILEX AQUIFOLIUM

A sweet holiday ornament for cakes as well as packages, this traditional evergreen adds a festive touch. With its shiny spiny leaves and scarlet red berries, it always reminds us of our happy holly days.

LEAVES

Roll out medium green dough moderately thin and cut with holly cutter. Thin edges on pad with ball tool and insert 30g green wire. With needle tool, point tips and mark center vein. Make 3 to 5 per sprig. Let dry. Dust dark green and brush with piping gel. Dust points red.

BERRIES

Roll an extra-small ball of red dough and insert a hooked 30g green wire. Indent center with umbrella tool. Make at least 5 per sprig. Brush with red piping gel. Let dry. With detail brush, paint indentation dark brown.

ASSEMBLY

Attach leaf to tip of a 22g wire. Add 2 or 3 berries with green tape. Then join leaves left and right. Dust stem burgundy.

Fiddlehead Fern

Whether piped in icing or sculpted in sugar dough, long curvaceous fiddleheads bring charm and movement to any floral design. The shape of its young fronds resembles the neck of a violin or fiddle. Most ferns uncoil in this manner. Described here is a variety called Cinnamon Fern because of its rusty coloring.

FERN

For a 3-4" (7-10cm) fern, roll an extra-large ball of green dough into a long tube with a bulbous end. With needle tool, draw a deep crease down center below wide end. Lay on pad and flatten slightly. With ball tool, thin and scallop left side of wide end. Curl to form fiddlehead. Insert 22g wire into stem. Let dry in soft S-curve. Dust dark green and glaze stem with piping gel. Sprinkle lightly with granulated sugar to texture. Let dry. Dust scallop cinnamon or rust.

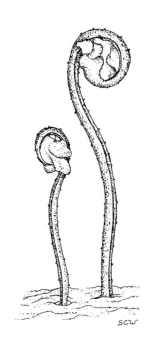

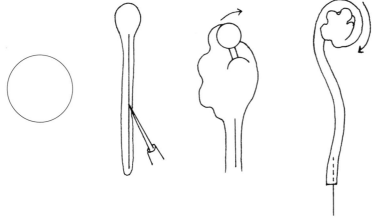

Well, fiddle-dee-dee!

"Wine and Song"
The marriage of families in wine and marble inspired this luscious and intoxicating design.

Grapes

VITIS

Dangling from the tiers of a wedding cake, glistening sugar grapes are visually intoxicating. Clusters of these light green, red or purple fruit are easy to make and add a luscious look. As a symbol of abundance, grapes are a fitting and festive decoration.

FRUIT

Roll yellow green dough into any size ball. Insert a hooked 30g wire. Let dry. Dust medium green and gloss with piping gel. With detail brush, paint a light brown dot in center. Make 20-25 balls of varying sizes per cluster. (For miniature champagne grapes, use small or extra-small balls.)

CLUSTER

Wrap tape to tip of a 26g wire and attach smallest grape. Continue down wire adding larger grapes. Increase length of stems as you build triangular cluster.

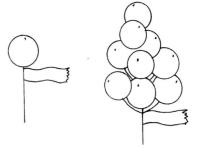

LEAVES

Roll out medium green dough moderately thin and press with veiner. Thin edges with ball tool on pad and insert a green 30g wire. Enhance center vein with needle tool. Let dry. Make 1 or 2 per cluster. Dust dark green and gloss with piping gel. Edge pink or red.

TENDRIL AND ASSEMBLY

Twist a length of green tape ¼" (7mm) wide and spin into a thread. Wrap loosely around handle of narrow paintbrush or dowel and slip off. Attach to cluster wire and add leaves.

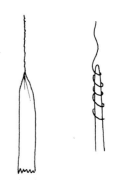

"Lovers Entwined"
Vines of ivy add movement and delicacy to this intricately woven wedding cake.

I v y

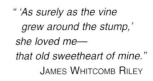
HEDERA

A trailing sprig of ivy helps form a delicate end to any floral spray. Whether dangling over tiers of a wedding cake or climbing down the sides of a basket of sugar flowers, ivy always brings movement and grace. A classic vine has several sizes of leaves and ends with a curly tendril.

LEAVES

Roll out green dough moderately thin. Press with leaf veiner. Make cut with any ivy, leaf, or petal cutter. (Many petal cutters can be used for leaves. For instance, pointed rose petal cutters make graceful teardrop-shaped ivy with wire in rounded end.) Thin edges with ball tool on pad. Insert 30g wire into base. Point tips with needle tool. Let dry. Dust center dark green and gloss with piping gel. Edge pink or red, depending on shade of green dough. Make at least 3 leaves of different sizes. Make all small and some medium sizes with brighter yellow-green dough to suggest newer, younger leaves.

VINE

For tendril, stretch a strip of floral tape at least 5" (13cm) long x ¼" (7mm). Twist to form thread and loosely wrap around a thin paint-brush handle. Slip off. Make several. Attach to tip of a long wire (any gauge) with floral tape. Continue down wire ½" (13mm) and add smallest leaf with a stem. Continue on adding leaves left and right increasing in size and interspersing tendrils. Dust vine reddish-brown leaving end green.

VARIATION

For variegated ivy, roll out medium green dough. Distress right edge with frill tool. Cover. Roll out cream dough thin and place jagged green edge halfway on cream. Roll doughs to join as shown. Proceed as above.

Ladybug

COLEOPTERA

COMMON NAMES: Lady Beetle, Lady Fly, Lady Bird

What a sweet accent this tiny insect makes when it lands on a sugar creation! A member of the beetle family, the ladybug is usually dressed in beige, orange, or red with a polka-dot pattern. The number of dots varies from bug to bug.

FORMING BODY

Roll a small ball of red dough into a stubby teardrop. Indent narrow end with the top of a #7 tip to form head. For eye, indent head twice with #3 tip. With needle tool, mark line down center of body, below head. For legs, cut stem of black stamen into 6 tiny lengths. Dip into glue and insert into side of body (as in drawing). Let dry.

"PATCH O' DILLYS"
Cheery daffodils stand tall in a bed of icing grass with a ladybug on her way home.

PAINTING

With detail brush, paint body (not head) with red piping gel. Let dry. Paint head and dots with black food color. Let dry. Use tweezers to bend legs downward and feet upward to bring your lovable ladybug to life.

Hint: Always use tweezers when placing sugar ladybug to avoid smearing.

Lunaria

"O Fortune,
 Variable as the moon,
 Always dost thou wax and wane"
 "Carmina Burana,"
 Twelfth-century Song

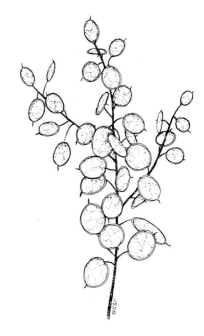

COMMON NAMES: Moonwart, Satin Flower, Honesty, Money Plant, Silver Dollar, Penny Flower

Dangling in the cool breezes of autumn, the silvery moonlike pods of this perennial herb delight the eye. Waxing, it produces fragrant white or purple flowers, followed by its familiar waning stage of opalescent wafer-thin seed pods. Many nicknames, as variable as the moon, have been "coined" because of its characteristic round, flat, and shiny appearance. *Lunaria*, named for the goddess of the moon, adds a shimmer of fantasy to cakes and arrangements.

FORMING PODS

Roll out dough moderately thin. Cut with circular or slightly oval cutter ½" (13mm) diameter. With rounded scissors, make a snip ¼" (7mm) long at edge. Carefully bend point out. With needle tool, mark a line around circumference of pod just inside edge. Insert a damp 30g wire opposite point, only ⅛" (4mm). On pad, dent surface several times with medium ball tool to ripple. Let dry. Dust edge and point light brown, then pearlize both sides strongly. Make at least 7 per stem of varying sizes, up to 1½" (4cm) in diameter.

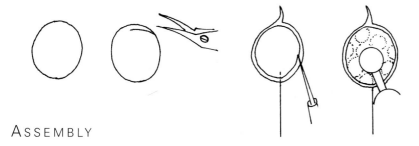

ASSEMBLY

Attach stem of smallest pod to tip of a 24g wire with floral tape. Continue down wire attaching pods in increasing sizes with a ½" (13mm) stem. Dust tape and stems light brown.

For branch, prepare 2 or more short stems. With a 22g wire, form main stem with 3-5 small pods at top. Then attach prepared stems left and right down wire.

Mistletoe

PHORADENDRON FLAVESCENS

The dreary cold of winter is often warmed by the custom of kissing underneath the mistletoe. Perhaps its paddle-shaped leaves formed in pairs suggested this tradition of coupling. Actually a parasitic evergreen, it flourishes on trees from New Jersey to Florida and produces poisonous translucent berries. A sturdy ornament, sugar mistletoe can be saved for years to come.

BERRIES

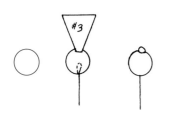

Work a touch of mint green food color into dough, keeping it almost white. Form an extra-small ball. Insert a hooked 30g green wire and indent other end with #3 tip. Push wire further into ball to raise indentation. Brush with piping gel to gloss. Let dry. With detail brush, paint tip light brown. Make 3-5 per sprig.

LEAVES

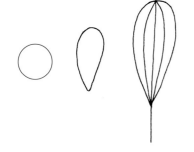

Form a small or medium ball of green dough into a long teardrop. Roll out flat, leaving point thick. Insert a 30g green wire into tip. With ball tool, thin edges on pad. Mark 3 lines with needle tool as shown. Let dry. Dust bluish-gray and edges dark green. Make 2 or 4 per sprig.

BRANCH BUDS

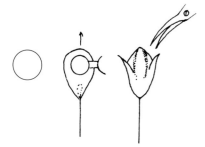

Roll a small ball of light green dough into teardrop. Insert 30g wire into point. With medium ball tool, roll outward to hollow center. Pinch tip to point. Make 2 snips with cuticle scissors. Let dry. Dust bluish-green at base and tips pink. Make 1 or 2 per sprig.

ASSEMBLY

Attach branch bud to tip of 22g wire with green tape. Join leaves left and right with berries at juncture. Move down stem 1" (25mm) and add another grouping.

Mushroom and Toadstool

Mother Nature's perky parasols pop up in every shape, color, and size imaginable. Usually, the edible mushroom has a wider cap, while its inedible neighbor, the toadstool, is shaped more like a closed umbrella.

MUSHROOM

For stem, roll a ball of dough into a thick tube. Snip both ends flat with scissors and insert hooked 22g wire halfway up. For cap, flatten a big ball of dough between palms, keeping center mounded. Indent with ball tool for stem attachment later. With exacto knife, cut concentric lines around indentation. Split edge here and there. Brush center with glue and place on top of stem. Let dry. Dust lines under cap brown. Dust stem and edge of cap light brown.

TOADSTOOL

Make stem as above but longer and thinner. For cap, insert ball tool into ball of dough to hollow and lengthen. On pad, scallop edges with ball tool. Brush glue inside and place on top of stem. Let dry. Dust top, stem, and edge of cap light brown.

Pussy Willow

The much-loved catkins of this North American willow tree prolif-erate on lengthy branches in early spring. Their silky and fuzzy appearance reminds us of our furry feline friends.

CATKINS

Roll a small ball of dough into a softly rounded teardrop. Insert a hooked 30g wire into pointed end. Let dry. Dust apple green up from base, leaving tip white, then pearlize. With reddish-brown food color, paint almond-shaped hull over base. Let dry. Make at least 7 per branch.

BRANCH BUDS

Roll a tiny ball of brown dough into a teardrop. Insert damp 30g wire into wide end. With needle tool, draw hip at base. Let dry. Dust darker brown. Make at least 5 per branch.

ASSEMBLY

Attach 2 branch buds piggyback to a tip of a 22g wire with green floral tape. Travel down wire ½" (13mm) or more and attach first catkin closely, with hull facing out. Finish by attaching alternately branch buds and catkins. Dust stem reddish-brown. Be careful not to discolor catkins.

Wheat

TRITICUM

Whether strewn at a bride's feet or worn in her hair as a crown, this golden grain has been used as a symbol of fertility since ancient times. These matrimonial traditions led to the baking of wheat cakes, predecessors of today's wedding cakes.

KERNELS

Cut tips off 25 white stamens. Roll an extra-small ball of golden yellow dough into a bead. Thread onto stamen. With needle tool, crease line down center. Make 25 per stalk.

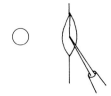

ASSEMBLY

Wrap tape around tip of a 22g wire. Attach kernel. Continue down wire joining 4 or 5 kernels in a row. Add 4 or 5 rows, with last row of 3. Dust golden yellow, then dark tan.

STALK

Roll out same dough thin and press with corn husk. With circular blade, cut a long, thin triangle. Brush middle of wire with glue and attach dough, bending tip back. Let dry and dust as before.

May your *wheat flourish*!

"Harvest Moon"

Preceding page: *Wheat, a symbol of abundance, is the inspiration for an extraordinary wedding design. Autumn's vivid colors are reflected in the flowers, fruits, and Pasha butterfly.*

AND OTHER SUGAR DECORATIONS

CROWING GLORY

FAN FARE

REINING BOWS

RIBBON BOUQUET

HOLIDAY BOW

PEACOCK BOW

FAVORING THE TABLE

PLACE CARDS

NAPKIN RINGS

NAPKIN SPRAY

PANORAMA EGG

HOLIDAY ORNAMENTS

GINGERBREAD HOUSE

"Crowing Glory"

Crowning Glory

Give someone the royal treatment and present them with this regal sugar crown, resting on a velvety pillow cake. An edible metallic powder performs a touch of alchemy by turning sugar into what appears to be gold.

DIAMOND POINTS

Cut 14 26g wires ¾" (2cm) long. Roll out golden yellow dough moderately thin and cut with large diamond cutter or use circular blade and template. Cut out center with Daphne or other small blossom cutter and poke out holes with #3 tip. Indent center of blossom with same tip and save. Insert wire into end and draw line inside edge with needle tool. Let dry slightly curved.

Hint: Lay inside large bowl to shape.

Make 7. Make 7 more blossoms for upper edge of crown. Prepare 7 small diamonds as above omitting cutouts. Let dry.

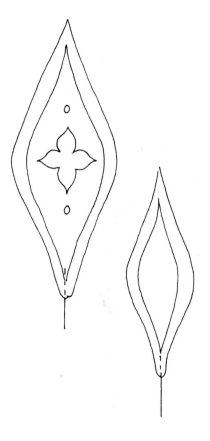

BAND AND ASSEMBLY

Roll out a large strip of dough ⅛" (4mm) thick. Cut out a band 1¼" (3cm) by 19" (54cm) long with circular blade. Crease line along sides with needle tool. Wrap around inverted 6" (15cm) cake pan to dry briefly. Remove and glue seam together. With needle tool, poke 14 holes along top edge of band, approximately 1½" (4cm) apart. Dampen wires and insert diamond points, alternating large and small. Attach blossoms in between points on top edge. When dry, paint with gold powder mixed with lemon extract.

Optional: To elaborate bottom edge, use tiny lace cutter or pipe delicate border with royal icing to attach to cake.

PILLOW CAKE

Carve off the top and bottom edges of a frozen 12" (30cm) square cake to round the sides. Cover with deep purple fondant and tuck bottom edges under. For upholstery effect, mark at least 16 deep creases outward from center to edge with needle tool. For button, flatten a large ball of fondant and attach to center with glue. With royal icing, pipe rope border along edge. For tassels, pipe long strands at each corner with "hair" tip. Pipe dot at top of tassel and paint gold when dry.

Sound the trumpets!

Fan Fare

Cause a stir by adorning a design with this fancy sugar creation.
Two different methods of construction are described here.

"Fancy Stringwork"
Above, tiny blossoms hide behind delicate strings of royal icing with sonia roses, freesia, and forget-me-nots gracing a Victorian fantasy.

"Fantasia"
Right, a simple bamboo pattern is piped behind moth and dendrobium orchids. On top an Oriental fan completes the theme.

Victorian Fantasy

This intricate design is formed by joining individual slats with a narrow satin ribbon.

SLATS

Roll out dough moderately thick. Cut with fan cutter. Make sure slits for ribbon are open and cleanly cut. Cut hole in bottom with #5 tip for wire assembly. Use any other tiny cutters or tips to elaborate fan design. Be sure cuts are placed consistently for each slat. Lay first slat next to each additional one to assure alignment. Let dry flat and perfectly straight. Make 15-18 slats.

Suggestion: Make a few extra in case of breakage during assembly.

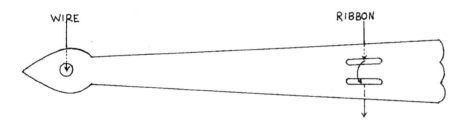

ASSEMBLY

Thread a 30g wire 6" (15cm) long through hole in bottom of slat. Simultaneously thread long, flexible ribbon ¼" (7mm) wide through open slits. Continue adding slats keeping ribbon taut between pieces. After last slat, twist ends of wire carefully together and cut off both ends of ribbon neatly. Leave ½" (13mm) tab. Attach both tabs to back of fan with royal icing. For standing display, make 2 triangles with dough as shown. Attach to cake surface and back of fan with royal icing. (The variation of coloring in pictured fan was achieved by using 9 graduated shades of dough, blue to white.)

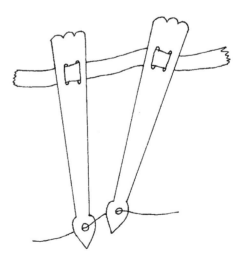

Oriental Fantan

Inspired by the open paper fans of the Orient, this variety is formed in one piece of sugar dough and is simpler to execute.

METHOD

Prepare template. Roll out dough medium thick and cover with template. Use exacto blade to cut out short edges and circular blade for longer ones. Remove template. With needle tool, mark lines down center of each *pointed* slat. Let dry. Using royal icing, overpipe edge of rounded slats with #1 or #2 tip. Attach tiny flower blossoms near top and pipe stems. Dust pointed slats pink. Paint square edge of fan, overpiping, and edges of flowers with nontoxic gold mixed with oil or lemon extract.

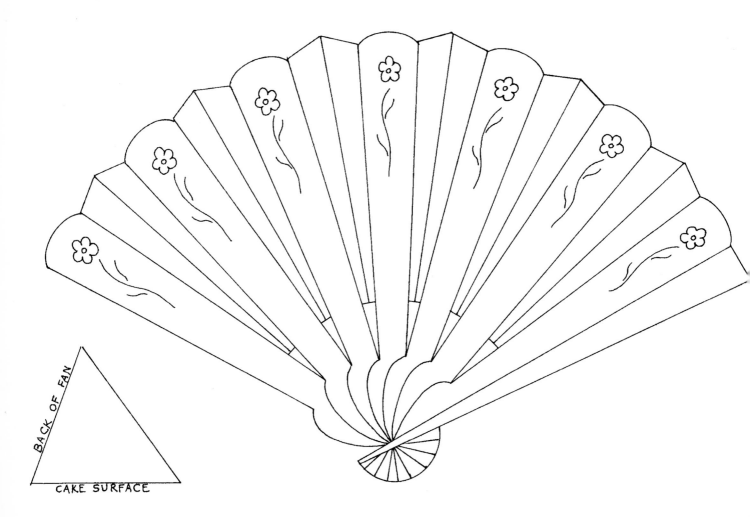

Reining Bows

Ribbon Bouquet

What a lovely pinnacle for a tiered wedding cake! Its pyramidic structure lifts the eye to a graceful point. Small and medium flowers are easily interspersed among the many loops to form a classic wedding bouquet.

PREPARING LOOPS

Roll out a large rectangle of dough moderately thin 7½" (19cm) wide. Cover with plastic wrap. With circular blade, cut out a strip ⅜–½" (1cm) wide by 7½" (19cm) long. With tracing wheel, mark stitches inside edge on both sides. Make loop with stitches out. Pinch and round ends together. Insert a 26g wire and lay straight on its side with loop open. Let dry. Cut out and loop 6 more strips 7" (17cm) long. Let dry with slight backward bend. Repeat for 6 more strips 6½" (15cm) long, drying them bending further backward.

ASSEMBLY

Attach floral tape to wire at base of largest loop. Attach 6 medium loops in a circle beneath it. Add smallest loops beneath and between previous row.

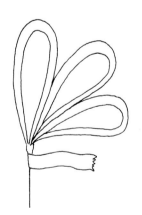

VARIATIONS

For satin ribbons, brush loops with pearl dust. For metallic effect, paint edge or entire surface with nontoxic gold, silver, or bronze dust mixed with vegetable oil or lemon extract. (Mixing with oil creates a brighter look than the extract but does not dry to the touch. It does, however, spread the powder more evenly and will go further.) For a more rounded bow, cut strips of equal lengths without bending to dry. To assemble, bend wires 45-90° before attaching to central loop.

"TYING THE KNOT"
Above, sugar ribbons gathered in a bow stream down the tiers of this radiant wedding cake.

"PASSIONATE LOVE"
Above right, close-up of ribbon bouquet.

Right, peppermint icing and red gum paste stripes cover a cake of holiday cheer.

Holiday Bow

LOOPS

First, place a dowel or rolling pin over the edge of a tabletop and secure other end with masking tape. Roll out red dough (or other desired color) moderately thin. Cut out Shape A in any size with a circular blade. Run tracing wheel along side edges. Slide over light dusting of cornstarch and loop around dowel or pin. Pinch ends together and snip off excess. Let dry until firm. Slip off and lay on side to dry completely.

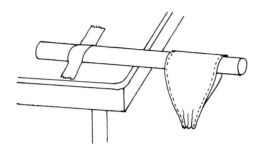

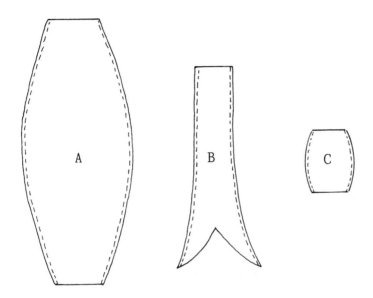

ASSEMBLY

For ribbons, make 2 cuts of Shape B and stitch as before. Pinch narrow ends and place next to each other, lifting points with fiber to curl. Brush glue at narrow ends and place loops on top to join. Cut out Shape C and stitch. Brush back with glue and place over middle of bow, tucking corners under. Let dry. For glossy look, brush with red piping gel. For satin, brush with red lustre dust.

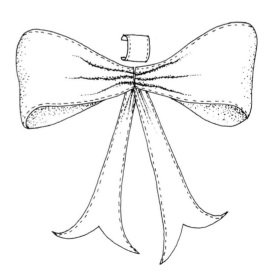

Peacock Bow

LOOPS

Prepare a dowel 1" (25mm) wide or rolling pin as for Holiday Bow. Roll out dough of desired color moderately thin. With circular blade, cut a 7" x 1" (18cm x 25mm) strip. Run tracing wheel along side edges. Slide over cornstarch. Loop around dowel and join ends with glue. Do not pinch. Let strip dry for at least 5 minutes and remove and place on side to dry. Make at least 7.

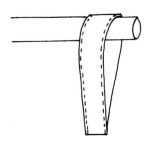

ASSEMBLY

Place 2 loops opposite each other. Pipe a dot of royal icing near base and place 2 more loops on top. Repeat and end by attaching single loop straight up. Let dry. To finish, brush with pearl or lustre dust.

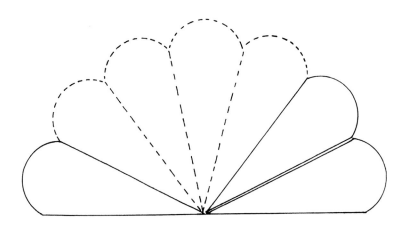

Favoring the Table

"Yours, Mrs. Stanley, will be sent to you on a tray. I'm using the dining room for my guests."

GEORGE S. KAUFMAN AND MOSS HART,
The Man Who Came to Dinner

Place Cards

Invite your guests to their places of honor in a most cordial way with sugar name cards. Easy to make and decorate, they add an original touch to any table setting. Adjust the shape, color, and lettering style to suit your occasion. Though edible, a sugar place card will most likely be saved as a memento.

FOLDED CARD

Crease an index card in half. Place on Styrofoam and set angle by inserting toothpicks. Roll out dough moderately thin and cut a rectangle 4" x 3" (10 x 7cm) with circular blade. Lightly mark line down center with needle tool. Lay over index card with crease along top edge. Let dry.

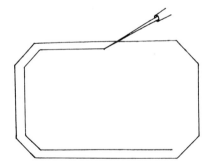

ENGRAVED CARD

Roll out dough moderately thin and cut rectangle. Remove corner points for beveled edges. With needle tool, mark line inside edge around card. Let dry.

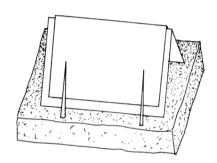

LACY PLAQUE

Roll out dough moderately thin. Cut with scalloped cutter or use template. Punch out holes or shapes inside edge using piping tips or tiny blossom cutters.

"WILD AT HEART"
Matching place cards and sprays
complement a florid design for an
intimate wedding celebration.

Below, ten place card designs.

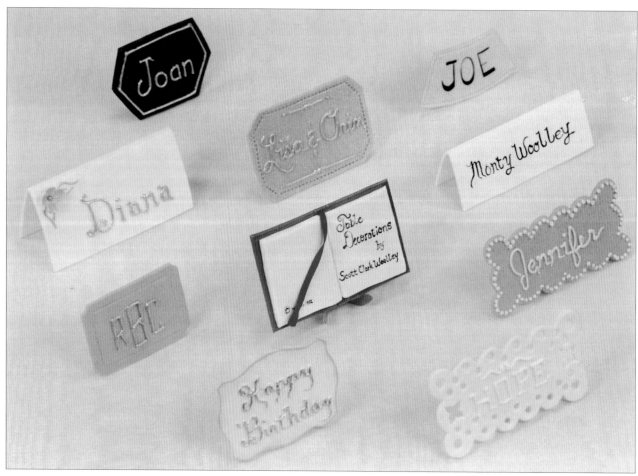

Inscriptions

Names may be added by piping with royal icing using fine decorating tips. For metallic effect, brush dried lettering with nontoxic metal powders mixed with lemon extract. Or simply paint the inscription with a detail brush using dark food paste color loosened with water.

Stand

Roll out dough moderately thin and cut 2 small triangles. Let dry. Pipe royal icing along dotted edges and attach to back of place card. Let dry. For smaller cards, 1 triangle will suffice.

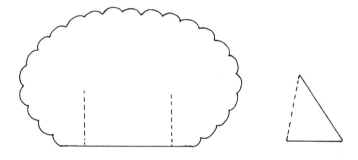

Other Shapes

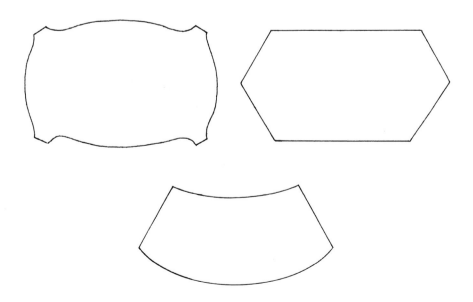

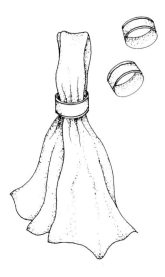

Napkin Rings

Liven up your table setting with colorful napkin rings that match the style or theme of your occasion. Party guests will marvel at these sturdy handmade favors. They'll never guess that they're made of sugar!

Twenty-three napkin ring designs.

Satin Ribbon

Roll out any color dough thick. With circular blade, cut a 1" x 5" (25cm x 13cm) strip. Run tracing wheel along side edges. Brush glue on short edges. Curl into a circle 1½"(4cm) in diameter and connect ends. Let dry. **Hint:** Draw a circle on paper to use as guide to form a perfect ring. Pearlize for satin sheen.

Fancy Filligree

Proceed as above and before curling, use small cutters and/or tips to punch out desired shapes or patterns.
   Variation: Pipe edges with royal icing to enhance cutout shapes.

Jungle Stripes

Roll out orange dough and quickly place black strips on top. Join pieces with rolling pin. Cut and shape as before.

Simple Ring

Form a tube of dough 5" (13cm) long. Snip ends flat and curl into ring, joining ends with glue.

Rope

Form 2 long tubes of dough. Twist together. Cut 5" (13cm) length and shape into circle. Attach ends with glue.

Wooden Band

Mix light and dark brown dough unevenly, dotting with small amounts of black. Roll out strip as before. With needle tool, draw 2 lines inside edges before curling.

Precious Stone

Mix several colors of dough unevenly. Cut strip as before and shape. Brush with Silver Snowflake Dust for glittery effect.
   Hints: For shiny look, brush with piping gel for plastic, polished stone, or wooden rings. For metallic effect, brush nontoxic metal powders using lemon extract for thorough drying.

Napkin Spray

Dress up a table setting with a spray of sugar flowers adorning each napkin. Untwisting a stem of flowers, buds, and leaves will delight each special guest. What a charming keepsake as well!

METHOD

Prepare 1-5 blossoms with buds and leaves. With tape, wrap pieces to a long 22g wire. Twist bottom of stem around napkin.

Rolled napkin with floral spray.

Panorama egg.

Panorama Egg

Peering through a window into a world of frolicsome bunnies rolling colorful eggs brings a smile to anyone's face. This large hollow egg is easily molded using granulated sugar and is decorated inside and out. If packed away safely each year, a panorama egg makes an enduring and endearing holiday centerpiece.

MOLDING

To form sugar egg, a set of two 9" (23cm) egg molds are necessary, which can be purchased at most cake decorating stores. First, preheat oven to 200°F. Mix 6 cups granulated sugar evenly with 2 egg whites. (For colored egg, add food paste color to egg whites before mixing.)   Pack mixture into molds ¼-½" (7-13mm) thick. For window, spoon out sugar 1¼" (3cm) in from narrow end, forming semicircle. Set in oven for 10-15 minutes until hard. Let cool and remove from molds.

DECORATING

For inner scene, prepare as many bunnies and colored eggs as desired using gum paste. With green royal icing, pipe grass with multiholed tip inside bottom half, up to edge. Place bunnies and eggs freely.

To join halves, pipe line of royal icing along edge of bottom half. Set other half on top. Overpipe seam with zigzag pattern, using tip #8. Add dots with tip #2 in green and white. For window, cut a circle of cellophane 3" in diameter. Attach to opening with dots of icing. Overpipe edge of circle with large pearls, using tip #8. With leaf tip #65, pipe green garland and attach prepared gum paste blossoms.

For lily of the valley bouquet, pipe 7 green stems with tip #3. Overpipe flowers in white with tip #81. Pipe white bow.

Holiday Ornaments

These sturdy sugar decorations make wonderful gifts for family and friends. For years they'll love unboxing these festive ornaments, recalling your sweet gesture. What jolly holiday treats!

EYE HOOKS

For each ornament, make a loop ⅜" (1cm) long in 26g wire. Twist ends several times tightly. Snip off excess.

Fourteen hanging ornaments.

Golden Sun

Roll out dough thick and cut 2 circles 1" and 2" (2 and 5cm) in diameter. With glue, attach small circle to center of larger one. Insert twisted end of eye hook into outer edge. With royal icing, pipe 12 straight lines with #2 tip from inner circle to edge. Then pipe 12 wavy lines in between. Let dry. Brush with gold powder mixed with lemon extract.

Silvery Moon

Roll out dough thick and make cut with circle cutter 2" (5cm) diameter. Move cutter to the side to cut out crescent shape. Insert eye hook near upper tip. Let dry. Brush with silver powder as before.

Gilded Leaf

Roll out dough thick and press with leaf veiner. Cut with any large leaf cutter. Insert eye hook into base of leaf. Let dry. Brush with gold or other nontoxic metallic powder.

Poinsettia

Make eye hook with 1" (25mm) stem. Roll out green dough moderately thin and cut with large calyx cutter. Mark center veins with needle tool. Roll out red dough and make second cut. With glue, attach to middle of green, placing stem of eye hook in between. Make 2 more cuts using medium and small cutters and attach to center. With #1 tip, pipe green and yellow dots in center with royal icing. Let dry.

"Parson Brown"

Build snowman with 3 different-size balls of dough. Glue together. Attach 2 small tubes for arms. Shape top hat with black dough and glue to head. Insert eye hook. Form mittens and boots and attach to body. Pipe features with royal icing. For scarf, cut thin strip of red dough and wrap around neck. Snip ends for fringe. Br-r-r-r-r!

Loving Hearts

Roll out dough thick and cut large heart. With smaller cutter, cut out center. Roll out red dough thick and cut small heart. Place inside large heart and insert eye hook into both. Let dry. Pearlize white heart and dust other with red lustre.

Shiny Bauble

Roll out dough moderately thin and cut 2 circles 2" (5cm) in diameter. Dry in cup formers. Join halves with royal icing, inserting eye hook at top. Cover seam with narrow strip of green dough. Pipe tiny red dots along edges with royal icing. Attach balls and beads under hook and at bottom. Brush with gold powder mixture. Pearlize.

Holly Wreath

Roll dough into narrow tube 6" (15cm) long. Shape into circle on wax paper, gluing ends. Insert eye hook. With tip #65, pipe dark green leaves around circle with royal icing. With #1 tip, pipe red dots for berries. Form tiny "Holiday Bow" and attach below hook with glue. Let dry.

Picture Frame

Roll out dough thick and cut 2 large circles. Cut out center of one with oval cutter. Insert eye hook into other. Trim photo or image to fit circle and secure with royal icing. (**Optional:** Cover image layer of cellophane for protection.) Glue second circle on top, positioning oval over image. Pipe details, such as date, greeting, or bordering.

Suggestion: Clip holiday images from old greeting cards, catalogs, or magazines. Or even paint your own!

To preserve ornaments, spray with thin coat of shellac to protect from dust.

Gingerbread House

Fanciful houses made of gingerbread and candy have charmed children and adults alike for centuries. What a joy it is to create your own holiday centerpiece that will entertain family and friends for years to come. This design combines royal icing, floodwork, and gum paste techniques to make the candy decorations, giving it a more realistic look. Wonder who shoveled the snow?

GINGERBREAD

Preheat oven to 350°F. (180°C, gas mark 4)
Cream together until light:

> $^1/_2$ *cup (115g/4oz) margarine or unsalted butter*
> 1   *cup sugar (200g/7oz caster sugar)*

Beat in:

> 1   *cup (330g/scant 12oz) light or dark molasses*
>   *(choice determines final color)*

In separate bowl, mix together:

> 5   *cups flour (625g/1lb 6oz plain flour)*
> 3   *teaspoons ground ginger*
> 2   *teaspoons ground cinnamon*
> $^1/_2$ *teaspoon ground cloves*
> 1   *teaspoon salt*
> 2   *teaspoons baking soda (bicarbonate of soda)*

Add dry ingredients alternately with:

> $^2/_3$ *cup (150ml/$^1/_4$ pint) water*

To form dough stiff enough to roll out.
Hint: If too stiff, add more water.

"Holiday Hermitage".

CUTTING AND BAKING

Lightly dust surface with flour and roll out dough ¼" (7mm) thick. Cover with templates for house and cut out shapes with circular blade. Lift carefully with metal spatula and place on nonstick or lightly greased cookie sheet. Check with template and reshape if necessary. Bake for 10-15 minutes until firm to the touch. Let cool completely on flat surface.

FLOODWORK DECORATIONS

Prepare patterns as described in Floodwork Setup. Pipe all lines with royal icing using tip #1. Flow icicles, shutters, and door with white icing, curtains green, and center of windows pale yellow for an inner glow. Don't forget the shutters on attic windows. Pipe 2 lace points for roof. Let dry 24 hours.

With detail brush, paint burning red candles and bows on curtains in all windows. Pipe lines over windows for panes.

GUM PASTE DECORATIONS

For Candy Cane Columns, twist together 2 long tubes of red and white dough and roll until smooth. Cut 2 columns 3" (7cm) long and let dry.

For the Lonesome Pine, form a tall cone with green dough. With leaf tip #68, pipe green royal icing branches starting at base. Let dry.

For Silly Snowman, see Holiday Ornaments. Form Welcome Mat with green dough and Snow Shovel with white. Paint curved rectangle with silver dust mixture and handle brown and black.

BUILDING HOUSE

The grounds for this gingerbread house need a 12" (30cm) square board. To assemble prepare loose royal icing. Place a back and side panel together at a 90° angle. With #6 tip, pipe line along bottom edges inside and up corner to join. Next add other side panel followed by front. Let dry briefly. Pipe along top edges and place roof panels. For chimney, assemble separately upside down joining corners with icing. Let dry briefly and attach to roof. Place porch in front. Place columns near edge and set porch roof on top, joining all pieces with icing.

For stone path, pipe main outline and individual stones with #2 tip. Flood stones with shades of gray. Pipe edge of board with #3 tip and flood snow with white icing. Let dry 24 hours.

FINISHING TOUCHES

Attach all windows and door with royal icing, then shutters. Along side edges of roof, attach strip of icicles. Don't worry if breakage occurs; snow on roof will cover. Spread icing thickly on roof with metal spatula and quickly pat smooth with palm dusted with cornstarch. Insert lace points at apex, front, and back.

With green royal icing, pipe shrubs, wreath, and garland, using leaf tip #65. Dot with red icing for berries and pipe bow on wreath with tip #1.

With #10 tip, pipe globs of snow on porch roof, chimney, corners of house, and on shrubbery.

Place and secure gum paste decorations with royal icing. For chimney smoke, use a tuft of cotton or cotton candy, if it's handy!

Close-up of gingerbread house.

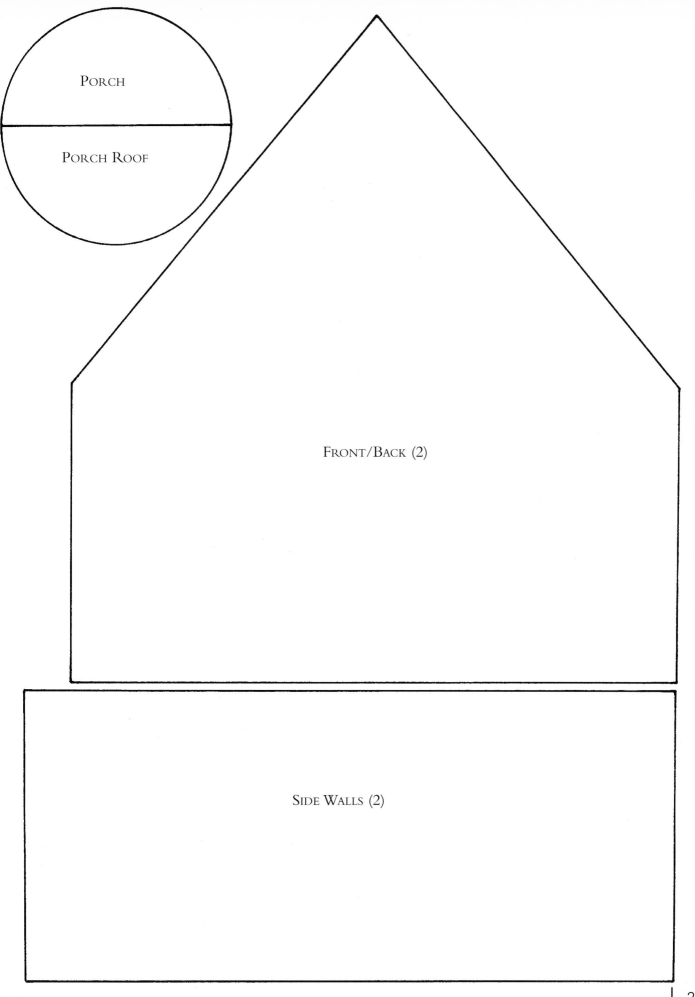

PORCH

PORCH ROOF

FRONT/BACK (2)

SIDE WALLS (2)

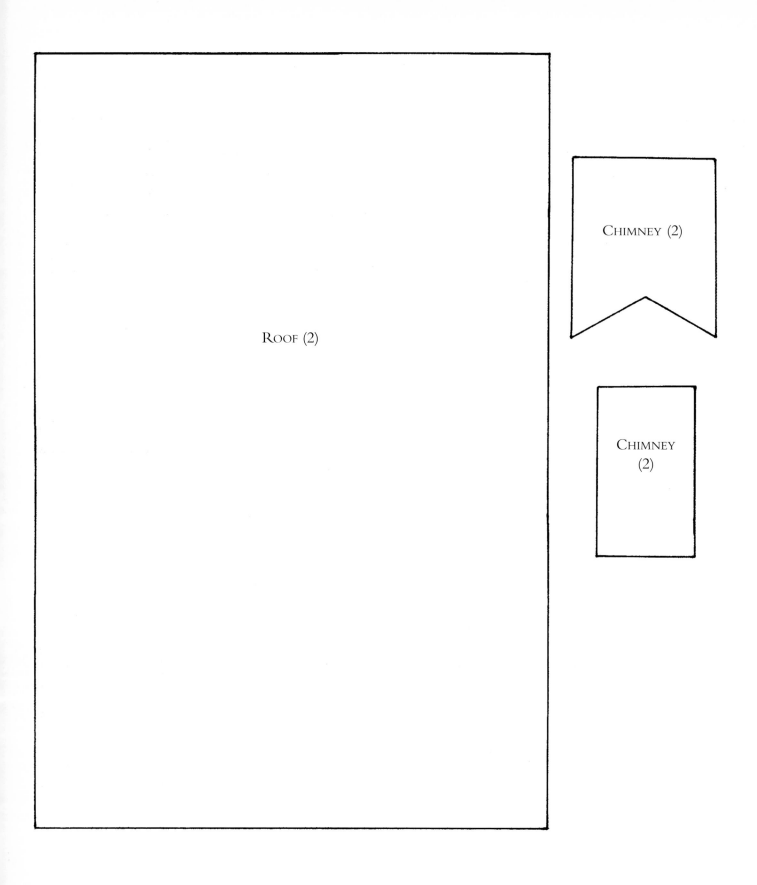

ROOF (2)

CHIMNEY (2)

CHIMNEY (2)

FLOODWORK PATTERNS

ICICLES

SHUTTERS

FRONT WINDOW

ATTIC WINDOWS

SIDE WINDOWS

DOOR

❖ ❖ ❖

PART FIVE

Preserving Sugar Art

Photographing the Work

Exciting photographs are essential to impress potential clients or employers. Here are some guidelines for achieving professional-looking photographs of a cake or other sugar work. Don't let all those hours of hard work be lost to the cake knife!

CAMERA

Cameras are made in large, medium, and small formats. The 35mm camera or small format is used by many professional photographers. It is lightweight and allows for interchangeable lenses with the advantage of 36 exposures per roll. For the photographs in this book, I used a 35mm camera with a zoom and macro lens attached for close-ups.

EQUIPMENT

A tripod is necessary to achieve clear and sharp images. It holds the camera still and maintains the desired angle and composition of the shot.

As a light source, I use 3 to 5 blue 250-watt photoflood bulbs with silver reflectors. These bulbs are inexpensive and work particularly well when shooting white wedding cakes. Keep in mind that this continuous light source can get very hot compared to using a flash so don't position them too close, and shoot quickly. Also, a small fan can keep the hot air moving away from cakes. This method enables you to see the lighting effect achieved *before* shooting.

If using a flash, bounce the light off the ceiling, wall, or photo umbrella to soften its effect. Using a flash straight-on will give a flat look to the shot and wash out some areas.

On the following page is a setup using 3 flood lamps. Generally, it's important to hang a light directly above object to pick up details and create shadow. If impossible, have someone hold a lamp above the cake.

FILM

For my photographs, I have used Daylight Color Print film ASA 100 and Slide Transparency film ASA 64. Both achieve accurate color reproduction when using blue bulbs. It is advisable to use both negative and slide film. Each has its purposes: prints are cheaper and are easily passed to clients while transparencies may be used for slide presentations or transferred onto videotape for other promotional purposes. Plus, your chances of getting a truly exciting shot greatly increase!

When developing, take your film to a reputable printer known for quality work. Quickie drugstore processing usually gives poor results. Printing film is a precise art form and even the most professional printers may print your work too light, too dark, or off color. Be sure you're happy with the final prints.

BACKDROPS

An appropriate backdrop for the object is an important consideration. Avoid colors that are too contrasting or absorb too much light. Whites, blues, and grays work well just as the sky makes a wonderful backdrop for everything on the earth. A roll of SuperWhite photographic paper can be painted to create a whole array of colors, textures, and effects. SuperWhite paper reflects back the most light and will not gray out as much as regular white paper. For a sky background, use an airbrush with water-based paints for a soft gradation of color. Speckled or marble effects can easily be done with brushes or small sponges.

Fabrics can offer a wide variety of looks. Have several colors and styles on hand and hold near the object to select the one that complements your work best.

STYLING

After choosing a backdrop, decide between a portrait or setting shot. A portrait shot emphasizes the object more than the setting. Tape paper or fabric to back wall and bring bottom forward onto tabletop for a seamless background without a horizon line.

Or, design a setting using a table, dressings, props, decorations, etc. Be aware not to clutter the scene with objects that will compete with the primary focus. Busy tablecloths or props may steal attention.

Prop ideas: candlesticks, wine or champagne glasses, knife sprays, sugar petals or flowers, rice, balloons, ribbons, bows, confetti, streamers, etc.

PORTFOLIO

A professional-looking album of previous work is essential for consultations or job interviews. For years, I've used two standard multi-ringed artist's portfolios 8½" x 11" and 11" x 14" (with plastic protective sheets. I replaced the black inserts with white art paper to improve the look. As with most illustrated books, photos are usually framed by white pages. A title page with pertinent business information is a good way to begin. Alternate enlargements and close-ups to keep the viewer's interest.

Don't say "Cheese," say "Cheesecake!"

Care

In order to save sentimental cake decorations or to display sugar works of art, be sure to keep pieces away from dust, moisture, and direct sunlight. Because of the fragile nature of this form, glass or Lucite boxes work well to protect them. Handled with care, sugar art will remain unchanged for many years, to delight the heart again and again.

For display, the background of a Lucite box may be covered with fondant or floodwork before attaching sugar art.

A glass dome and base for protecting sugar work.

Dear Mother Earth,

Living in New York City for the last nineteen years, away from the green grass and rolling hills of my childhood, I have come to appreciate your splendor. You express yourself in such limitless variety, ever offering delights to behold. You have freely shared yourself, allowing me to experience a life full of wonder, of self-discovery and learning.

Oh! You ill-treated nurturer whose unconditional love ever flows. Be assured that this expression of gratitude is but one drop in the stream to come. As a child, I thrilled at chasing butterflies. Now, with adult and belated reverence, I dare to capture them only in sugar.

A student of Nature,

SCOTT CLARK WOOLLEY

Glossary

AIRBRUSH: An artist's paint gun using an air pump to spray paint or food coloring finely and evenly. Excellent for making backgrounds.

BACKDROP: Fabric or paper background that is either draped or hung smoothly.

BUD: The first stage of a growing branch, leaf, or flower.

CALYX: The outer protective covering of a flower, which folds back when open in segments called sepals.

CASCADE: A continuous flow of decorations that tumble down from level to level.

COCOA: Powder of roasted cacao beans, when added to oil makes an excellent substitute for processed chocolate.

CONFECTIONERS' SUGAR: Powdered granulated sugar used to make icings, gum paste, fondant, etc.

CORNSTARCH: A powdered maize used as a thickener in cooking and to dry gum paste when working.

COUPLER: A two-piece device placed in piping bag allowing speedy interchange of decorating tips.

CREAM OF TARTAR: Potassium bitartrate; a white powder used to hold beaten egg whites and to harden flowed sugar.

DOTTED SWISS: Texture effect made by dotting surface area.

FLOODWORK: Precise and exact decorations made by flowing liquefied royal icing within piped borders.

GELATIN: Ingredient of gum paste, this protein strengthens the sugar work.

GUM ARABIC: Powdered resins of the acacia tree, when mixed with water makes gum glue, a substitute for egg white as an adhesive.

GUM TRAGACANTH: Powdered resin that is essential ingredient for gum paste to ensure its elastic qualities.

LACE POINTS: Royal icing piped filigree that extend past cake.

LATTICE WORK: Royal icing effect where lines are piped in a crisscross design.

PETALS: The outermost segments of a flower.

PISTIL: Female part of flower that bears the seed and houses the stigma and ovaries.

PIPE: To squeeze icing from a bag through a decorating tip.

SEPAL: One segment of a calyx.

SPATULA: Broad, flat metal utensil used to spread icing smoothly and evenly.

STAMENS: Male part of flower made up of filament and anther, which carries the pollen. Premade stamens for floral work may be purchased at cake decorating suppliers, or make your own.

THROAT: Trumpetlike center of a flower.

THROAT FORMER: Object used to shape and dry orchid centers.

TIER: To stack cakes of graduating sizes.

TIER SEPARATORS: Constructed supports that separate stacked cakes.

TONGUE: Sausage-shaped protuberance near the center or top of orchid throat

TURNTABLE: Revolving cake stand for easier decorating.

ZEST: Thin, colored outer coating of citrus fruit, not to be confused with thick, white pulp, which is bitter. The outer rind that carries the oil extracts.

Sources and Suppliers

"And the day came when the risk to remain, tight in a bud was more painful, than the risk it took to blossom."
—Anaïs Nin

Scott Clark Woolley
Michael G. Farace
171 West 73rd Street, Studio 9
New York, NY 10023
(212) 362-5374

Bridge Company
214 East 52nd Street
New York, NY 10022
(212) 688-4220

New York Cake & Baking Center
44 West 22nd Street
New York, NY 10010
(212) 675-2253

Broadway Panhandler
477 Broome Street
New York, NY 10013
(212) 966-3434

Meadows Chocolate & Cake Supplies
110-16 Liberty Avenue
Richmond Hill, NY 11419
(718) 835-3600

Sunflower Sugar Art
P.O. Box 780504
Maspeth, NY 11378
(914) 227-6342

Country Kitchen
3225 Wells Street
Fort Wayne, Indiana 46808
(219) 482-4835

Sweet Celebrations
7009 Wasington Avenue South
Edina, Minnesota 55439
(800) 328-6722

Creative Cutters
561 Edward Avenue, Units 1 & 2
Richmond Hill, Ontario, Canada L4C 9W6
(416) 883-5638

Pearl Paint (Art Supplies)
308 Canal Street
New York, NY 10013
(212) 431-7932

American Cake Decorating Magazine
811 West Maple Avenue
Sterling, Virginia 20164
(703) 430-2356

Mailbox News (Cake Decorating Magazine)
P.O. Box 16208
Minneapolis, Minnesota 55416
(612) 928-3025

Index

t

v

w

z